Write Grants, Get Money

By Cynthia Anderson

Cataloging-in-Publication Data

Anderson, Cynthia, 1945-
    Write grants, get money / by Cynthia Anderson.
       p. cm.
    Includes bibliographical references and index.
    ISBN 1-58683-025-2 (perfectbound)
      1.   Library fund raising—United States. 2. Proposal writing in library science—United States. 3. Proposal writing for grants—United States. 4. School library finance—United States. 5. Instructional materials centers—United States—Finance. I. Title.

Z683.2.U6 A53 2001
025.1'1'0973—dc21   2001038555

Published by Linworth Publishing, Inc.
480 East Wilson Bridge Road, Suite L
Worthington, Ohio 43085

5 4 3 2 1

Table of Contents

Acknowledgments ix

Introduction xi

Chapter 1: Identify the Need and Make a Plan 1
       Picture Your Dream 2
       Get Specific: Component Dreams 2
       Share the Dream 2
   Prepare for the Journey 3
       Visualize 3
       Write a Mission Statement 4
       Start a Resume 4
       Think Outside the Box 4
   What About Library Technology? 5
       E-Rate 5
       Technology Plan 5
       Cautions 6
   Needs Other Than Technology 6
       Collection Development 6
       Handicap Accessibility 6
       Special Programs 7
       Facility Needs 7
       Furniture 7
       Environment 7
       Memorials 8
       Workshops 8
   Getting Started 8
       Enter a Contest 9
       Think Solid, Not Earthshaking 9
       Strive for Action, Not Perfection 9
   Project Objectives 10

Chapter 2: Go Where the Grants Are 11
   Organize Your Research 12
   Some Tips as You Search for Funding Sources 12
       Stay Flexible 12
       Make Contacts 12
       Start Close to Home 13
   Types of Grants 13
       Foundations 13
           Independent or Private Foundations .13
           Company-Sponsored Foundations 14
           Community Foundations 14

Table of Contents *continued*

Government Funds 14
Resources to Help Find Grantors 15
    Internet Searches 15
    Directories 16
    Journal and Newsletter Searching 17
    Search Tips 17
Start Your Search Close to Home 21

Chapter 3: Read Grants and Form a Writing Team 23
    Contest Judge 24
Reviewing Grants 24
    Local Foundations 25
    State Grants 25
    Federal Grants 26
A Grant Proposal Reader's Responsibilities 27
    Learn from Reading Grant Proposals 28
Internal Review Team 28
Build a Grant-Writing Team 28
        Reader 29
        Abstract Writer 29
        Number Cruncher 29
        Researcher 29
        Statistician 29
        Shopper 29
        Proofreader 30
        Veteran 30
        Editor 30
        Key Communicator 30
        Delivery Person 30
        Copy Maker 30
        Pace Keeper 31
    Meet with Your Team 31
Grant-Writing Process 32

Chapter 4: Read the Fine Print 33
    First Reading 33
    Second and Third Readings 34
    Make Copies 35
Getting Ready to Write 35
    Save as You Go 36
    Call for Clarification 36

Table of Contents *continued*

Assess Your Proposal 37
    Read Some Winning Grant Proposals 37
Proposal Letter 38
Multiple Submissions 38

Chapter 5: Parts of the Proposal 39
Cover Letter 39
Title Page 40
Table of Contents 41
Abstract, Project Summary, or Executive Summary 41
Statement of Need 41
Goals and Objectives 43
Plan of Action 43
Budget 45
    Phases 45
    In-Kind 45
    Categories 45
    Estimate Accurately 46
    Make It Look Good 46
    Salaries 46
    Other Costs 46
    Make Changes Carefully 46
    Multiple Funding Sources 47
    Be Honest 47
    Use the Generic 47
    Cautions 47
Personnel 47
    Credentials 48
    Job Descriptions 48
    Resumes 48
    Biographical Sketches 48
Evaluation 49
    Formative or Summative 49
    Evaluating Technology 49
    Test Resources 50
    Evaluation Methods 50
    Interim Reports 51
    Evaluation Consultation 51
    Review Other Evaluation Components 51
Time Line 51
Dissemination 51
Sustainability 52

Table of Contents *continued*

Letters of Support 52
Certification and Signatures 53
Attachments, Supporting Documentation, and Appendixes 53
Sample Grant Proposals 54

Chapter 6: Speak Clearly 55
    Hook Your Reader from the Beginning 55
Define Terms 56
    Spell out Acronyms the First Time 56
    Avoid Jargon 56
Make It Simply the Best 57
    Avoid Redundancy, Cliches, and Fluff 57
    Find Synonyms 57
    Provide Examples 57
    Consider Your Reader 58
Use a Consistent Style and Format 58
    Find a Voice 58
    Speak Clearly 58
    Transition Words and Phrases for Coherence 58
Use the Language of the Grantor .59
Describe or State Precisely 59
Be Compelling and Fresh 59
Appearance Does Matter 60
    Graphics 60
    White Space 61
    Lists and Headings 61
    Spacing and Margins 61
    Font, Type Size, and Pagination 62
    Avoid Fancy 62
Plan Ahead 62

Chapter 7: Edit Until It Hurts 65
    Read, Reread, Write, and Rewrite 65
    Title It 65
    Headings and Lists 66
Revise It for Mechanics and Content 66
    Flesh It out 66
    Give It Punch 66
    Be Specific 68
You Can't Overdo Proofreading .68
Two Essentials: An Editor and a Proofreader 69

Table of Contents *continued*

Follow Directions to the Letter 69
   Checklist 70
   Checking the Budget 70
   Signatures 70
   Appendixes 71
   Cover Letter 71
   Copies 71
   Assembly 72
   Mailing 72
   Congratulations! 72

Chapter 8: Turn Rejection into Success 73
  Be Professional 73
   Notify Your Team 74
   Thank Participants 74
  Reasons for Rejection 75
  Learn from the Experience 77
   Feedback Helps 77
   Take a Class 77
   Read a Winner 78
  Try Again 78
   Revise and Recycle 78
   Apply to More Than One Grantor 79

Chapter 9: Celebrate and Share 81
   Elation, Then Letdown 81
  Get the Word Out 82
   Share the Limelight 82
   Keep a Scrapbook 82
   Share Within Your School 83
     Posters 83
     Bookmarks 83
   Share In the Local Community 83
     Press Releases 83
     News Conferences 83
     Newsletters 83
     PTA Meetings 83
   Share Among Your Peers 84
     Associations 84
     Journals 84
     Articles 84

Table of Contents *continued*

Share in Your Region and Beyond 84
 Project Fact Sheet 84
 Brochures 84
Once the Project Is Underway 84
Take Stock 86

Chapter 10: Follow Through 87
Getting Started 87
 Keep Records 88
 Budget 88
 Reporting 88
 Final Report 89
 Oversight Committee 89
Build a Relationship 89
 Site Visit 89
Evaluation 90
After the Project 90
 Extensions 90

Appendix A: Selected Works on Grants and Funding 93

Appendix B: U.S. Department of Education Technology Programs 105

Appendix C: Glossary 109

Appendix D: U.S. Department of Education Grant and Contract Forms 116

Appendix E: Top 10 U.S. Foundations by Total Giving 118

Appendix F: Sample Grant Proposal Format 119

Appendix G: Sample Resume 120

Appendix H: Directory of State Humanities Councils, Spring 2000 125

Appendix I: Technology Inventory 132

Appendix J: Sample Brochure: Shawnee Mission Education Foundation 133

Appendix K: Listservs for School Librarians 135

Appendix L: Sample Budget 137

About the Author 139

Index 140

Table of Figures

Chapter 1:   Figure 1:1   Big Dream 3
                      Figure 1:2   Mission Statement 4
                      Figure 1:3   Winning Proposals .... .10

Chapter 3:   Figure 3:1   Grant Writing Process .... .32

Chapter 5:   Figure 5:1   Title Page .... .40

Chapter 6:   Figure 6:1   Statistical Graph .... .60

Acknowledgments

I would like to thank my friends Terry Wintering, Charlotte Davis, and Elaine Crider for their immeasurable help in writing and preparing the manuscript for this book. Thanks to my daughter-in-law, Brooke Anderson, for her charming pen-and-ink drawings, to Dr. Beverly Nichols for sharing an excerpt from a winning grant, and to Carolyn Hoffman for sharing her resume with us. Thanks to the many school librarians, educators, granting organizations, and grant writers who shared their experience, knowledge, and good ideas with us.

Introduction

With just a little help from resources and contacts, any school library media specialist can write a winning grant proposal. *Write Grants, Get Money* was written to provide just such assistance to school library media specialists. This volume offers help to those who want to write grants in order to provide technology and other necessary and creative materials and services for their library media centers.

After writing or collaborating many winning grants and sharing grant-writing strategies at conferences and seminars, the author was asked to share those strategies in a book for school librarians. The purpose of *Write Grants, Get Money* is simple: to help school librarians get grant money for their schools. All school librarians who want more for their libraries than their budgets allow should have a copy of *Write Grants, Get Money*. This K–12 resource was written exclusively for school media specialists who need tips on finding funding and collaborating with others to write grant proposals to enhance their school library programs and facilities. This easy-to-read, to-the-point guide is a practical tool targeted specifically at the overworked, underfunded school librarian. The author is a practitioner who has tailored a wealth of information to help busy school media specialists acquire the technology and other materials they need to achieve their dreams.

Grant writing can seem daunting and mysterious. For some people, the hardest part of writing a grant proposal is cracking the ice and putting their toes in the chilly waters of grant proposal writing. Once they make that first attempt and write a proposal, each subsequent effort seems a little easier. Their confidence grows.

For others, getting larger and more complex grant funding seems out of reach. No matter where the reader is on the grant-writing continuum, she will find the information in this book practical and useful.

Write Grants, Get Money is a valuable asset to the school library media specialist who wants to provide more for the students in his school by easing into the field of writing grants. The book includes up-to-date resources and writing and editing tips, as well as the encouragement librarians need to start or continue writing winning grant requests.

The book is conveniently arranged in chapters covering the topics about which most potential grant writers need more information. From getting an initial idea for a grant, to researching the details and making a plan, to finding funding sources, the book outlines the entire grant application process. Here, the novice will find advice on forming a grant-writing team, then actually writing, editing, and proofreading the proposal. The book offers grant submission tips and information on implementing the grant that results from a successful proposal. *Write*

Grants, Get Money concludes with a trio of further resources in the appendixes: a glossary, an index, and a bibliography.

School librarians will find this book useful if they have never written a grant before, if they are veteran grant writers, or if they are somewhere in between. They'll find wisdom shared by school library media specialists from all over America who have written winning grant proposals and want to help their colleagues do the same. A common characteristic of outstanding school librarians is a constant striving for more technology, better programming, and more timely materials for the media center. This book will give the resourceful librarian the edge when applying for grant funding, and it can be used time and time again as a reference resource.

The following chapters will help the reader develop a broad, comprehensive plan for the future of the media center and identify needs that might be met by grant money. It will encourage the reader to become a grant reviewer in order to understand the grant-writing process and what makes a grant proposal succeed.

The book focuses on putting a grant-writing team together and then actually writing the grant. From reading the fine print to editing well, the reader will find practical guidance on grant writing and proposal submission. Definitions and examples, or sources for examples, of the sections of a grant proposal are included.

The reader will gain insight on what to do if the grant proposal is not funded and tips on how to proceed when the grant is funded. Appendixes include a bibliography of Web sites, journals, and books on grant writing. This meat-and-potatoes approach will answer questions, furnish necessary resources, and inspire the reader to get started or continue writing grant-winning proposals for the media center.

Write Grants, Get Money is not a dissertation, nor is it based on scholarly research. It is written from the experience of a grant-writing practitioner studying in the school of hard knocks. Readers should feel free to experiment with the advice or methods suggested and make them their own. The author is not a professional grant writer nor does she have any plans to quit her day job. She is just an educator who wants to share the benefits that come from writing winning grant proposals.

Chapter 1

Identify the Need and Make a Plan

One who takes small steps goes fast.

—Anonymous

Remember the line from the song in the musical *South Pacific*? "You gotta have a dream, if you don't have a dream, how you gonna have a dream come true?" Did you know that J.K. (Joanne Kathleen) Rowling dreamed of writing a series of books about a kid named Harry Potter? Her dream came true, in part, according to *Scholastic.com*, through a grant from the Scottish Arts Council (<www.scholastic.com/harrypotter/author/index.htm>). Grants can be the touch of magic you need to help you make your dream for your media center come true.

But before your dream can come true, you have to identify it. Time spent dreaming the big dream for your library is time well spent. If you, like Harry Potter, had a magic media-center wand, what would you wish for? What is your "if dreams came true" vision for your media center? Let your imagination flow. Picture your ideal program and facility. What are students doing? What does the facility look like? What resources are available for your students and staff?

You will need to dream both broadly and specifically. You will need a clear vision of the big picture and zoom shots of the specifics.

Picture Your Dream

Cut pictures of your ideal equipment from catalogs and post them with magnets on your bulletin board or file cabinet. Write a paragraph or two describing your dream. Consider buying a journal and giving yourself permission to dream impossible dreams in it. I like to use artists' sketchbooks from the art supply store because they don't have lines that make me feel compelled to fill them all before turning the page. I embellish the cover with rubber stamps, quotes, and trinkets to personalize it. I jot down ideas, sketches, and short paragraphs about things I can envision for the future. It gives me a delicious feeling, rather like being a child and thinking of all the possibilities out there in the world.

If you don't dream of what could be, you will be forever frozen in the status quo. Let yourself dream; it's good for your spirit.

Get Specific: Component Dreams

Once you have a mental picture of your big dream, you need to pull it apart into smaller component dreams and fill in the details. One of those components would make the perfect starting place for writing your first grant proposal. Apply for grants that target one or two specific goals or areas. Your chances will be better than if you start out asking for the moon. Later in your grant writing career you may tackle multi-year, complex federal grants, but I recommend keeping it simple to start.

It's important to have the big-picture dream, but keep in mind that writing a grant is a large undertaking and cannot be done in a day. It might even take an entire school year. Your big-picture dream may take a full career to accomplish, while one component of that dream may take only a school year to achieve. See Figure 1:1

Share Your Dream

Begin to seek support for your dream. Share your vision with your principal. Sharing with your principal or supervisor can be very helpful and should even be mandatory. First of all, she needs to be in your loop and support your dream. Second, if your principal or supervisor knows what you are dreaming, she can sometimes help you make your dream come true. Your principal may have capital funds remaining at the end of the budget year and might be willing to purchase a digital camera for the media center if she is aware that you want one. Or maybe she has enough for the software, disks, or carrying case you need. Every little bit of funding inches you forward toward your ideal program.

Share your vision with your colleagues. You never know who might be in a position to share your dream with someone who could connect you with a potential funding source. Bring your dream alive by having a planning session with your media-center Dream Team. Your Dream Team could include your library aide or clerk, and interested and supportive teachers, parents, and library volunteers. Getting early buy-in is critical to the success of your long-range plan. Your team must be on the same page with you if you plan to reach for the stars together. Never underestimate the power of a team of educators with a clear mission.

If your principal or supervisor agrees with you, share your dream with students, staff, and parents. Build community support for your vision for your media center. You never know when opportunity might come knocking at your media center door.

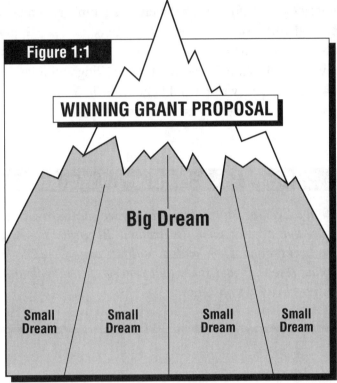

Figure 1:1

WINNING GRANT PROPOSAL

Big Dream

Small Dream **Small Dream** **Small Dream** **Small Dream**

Prepare for the Journey

Start keeping a journal in which you record your wishes and dreams for your media center. Allow yourself to be childlike in your journal. Don't let your grown-up self inhibit you. It doesn't matter if your dreams might be hard to achieve. What matters is that you give yourself license to brainstorm in an uncensored way. Carry your journal around with you, but don't share it with anyone who might rain on your parade. Put it beside your bed at night, just in case your subconscious solves a logistics problem for you or comes up with an ace idea. You don't have to confine your dreams to just your media center, either. If you want to attend a summer institute in storytelling, put that in your journal.

Visualize

Visualization is a powerful strategy. Picture yourself at the circulation desk with your new state-of-the-art check-out computer. Picture your high school students seated on those teak garden benches as they read periodicals in the new garden reading area of your library. Cicero said, "Anyone who has a library and a garden wants for nothing."

Write a Mission Statement

Do you have a mission statement for your library? Does your school have a mission statement? One of the things you will need as you apply for your grant is a statement of beliefs or a mission statement. While you are dreaming about what you would like your library to be, it would be a good time to start developing your mission statement. A mission statement is a simple statement expressing what you are about and what you want your library to be.

Start making notes in your journal. Write down words or phrases that express your ideals. After a few weeks of writing a note or two each day, take time to read what you have written and begin to edit. Your mission statement can be as short as one or two sentences that express succinctly what your library vision is all about.

Figure 1:2 Evening Star School Library Mission Statement

In the Evening Star School library we shall draw a circle and make sure that every student fits inside it. Regardless of race, gender, ability or background, each student will feel empowered to learn, thrive, read, research, and study in an energy-filled, technology-rich, supportive environment.

Start a Resume

If you don't have a current resume, begin making notes about your credentials. You will need a resume to include with your proposal or letters of inquiry. Where did you earn your college degrees and in what years? Where have you worked? What leadership positions have you held? Have you been PTA president or treasurer? What is your current job title and what are your duties and responsibilities? Get started writing a resume or curriculum vita sheet that will tell the grant-makers who you are. See Appendix G for a sample resume of a school library media specialist.

Think Outside the Box

Use this technique when you are dreaming big for your library media center. What would your library program look like if you put problem-based learning at the center of your lessons? What would the students be doing differently? What technology would you need to allow that to happen? How could you help your students take a more active role in their own learning? You may have some ideas that you have not seen in practice. That is okay. That is what makes one grant proposal stand out against another. Unique ideas, presented in a colorful way, may be just what it takes to get your grant funded.

When you think about writing a grant, have no fear. At least, have little fear. You have hard-earned degrees, you have written substantive research papers, and you teach people how to do research. You can write a winning grant proposal. There is money there for the asking. You can do it! So get started.

Developing a comprehensive, long-range plan for your media center is worth your while. There are several areas in your library that you could consider when you are looking at a long-range dream. Several facets of your program and facility have potential for enhancements. Read journal articles, take field trips, attend conferences, and visit with colleagues for ideas.

What About Library Technology?

E-Rate

One of the first steps you may want to take is to find out if your school district has a long-range technology plan. If your district has ever sought E-rate funding, there is probably an existing technology plan because that is one of the requirements to qualify for the E-rate. The E-rate is a federal fund to help schools and libraries get affordable access to the Internet. See if you can find that technology plan, and read it. It may include your school district's vision for the future of technology in your library, in your school, and in your district. For more information about the E-rate, visit <http://www.edlinc.org>.

Technology Plan

Consider developing a long-range district technology plan if you don't already have one. To write a district-wide technology plan, you'll need to involve your superintendent and other administrators. If a committee is forming to write your district technology plan, volunteer to serve on it. Not only will you have a chance to give your input, you will see from the beginning what the long-range dreams are for your schools.

Make your long-range technology vision specific so that you are ready to act when you have the opportunity. Take inventory of what you have; then you can make a long-range plan for computer replacement. A sample technology inventory sheet for you to use is included in Appendix I of this book.

As you make your long-range plan, prioritize your wishes and estimate the school year during which you would like to acquire the equipment. Although you may not be able to replace all your technology with grant money, you will not have wasted your effort by making a replacement plan. You may be in the right place at the right time if you have done your homework, prioritized your needs, and made a time line for replacement and enhancement of your technology.

Cautions

As you put together a plan for technology, observe a few cautions:

- Seek help when you need it.
- Build budget room in your proposal for price changes.
- Build in funds for forgotten cables, tapes, and the like.
- Make sure equipment pieces are compatible with one another.
- Follow district and state guidelines about purchasing, once you have your funds.
- Consider building in funds for installation and maintenance.
- Go see what you are requesting before you request it.
- Make sure you have the required power and data drops.
- Ask questions and take the advice of experts.

Needs Other Than Technology

Technology is not the only game in grant-writing town. Consider other areas as you envision your ideal library.

Collection Development

Do you need to acquire a variety of materials about cultural diversity? Is there a Rainbow Coalition in your community that funds efforts to promote understanding and harmony in your neighborhood or city? Your need to acquire multicultural materials may match their mission. Call them and see what grant monies might be available.

Are you planning to offer e-books to your patrons? How will you fund that? Tell your principal about your ideas. Do you have special collections— other languages, diversity, special needs, or classroom collections or archives—that might be enhanced by a grant?

Handicapped Accessibility

Do you need funding to bring your media center into compliance with the Americans with Disabilities Act? Does your school need an elevator so that all students can access the library? Computer tables and other furniture that is accessible from a wheelchair? A new circulation desk or modifications to the present one to make it wheelchair-accessible?

Special Programs

Consider writing a grant proposal for

- A program to serve young mothers,
- After-school activities,
- Multicultural events, or
- Mentoring programs.

Facility Needs

Do your younger students need a reading loft? Does your school need a faculty work area in the library for teachers who, because of space constraints, cannot be in their classrooms during their planning periods? An educational software company's foundation might be interested in funding such a project.

Furniture

Would a rocking chair make your story area more appealing? Do you need to replace your makeshift board-and-brick shelving with sturdy new shelving? Furniture needs to consider include

- Shelving,
- Circulation desk,
- Tables and chairs,
- Lounge furniture,
- Media storage equipment, and
- Computer furniture.

Environment

Perhaps there's a feng shui expert on staff who wants to give you sage advice on increasing the harmony, learning, and circulation in your library, or maybe your library just needs a face-lift. Your local home decorating center may be your fairy godmother. Do you just need a coat of paint, or do you need the whole nine yards of new blinds, paint, and carpet? Do you want lamps for ambient lighting or display cases to highlight student artwork? Would a drinking fountain improve concentration, increase traffic? Some furnishings to consider are

- Display cases,
- Artworks,
- Lamps and other lighting,
- Blinds or shades,
- Flooring, and
- Paint or wall treatment.

Memorials

When a community has lost a well-loved teacher, student, or parent, they wish to pay some lasting tribute to that person. The library is well suited to house a memorial, and grant money can be a way to provide it.

Workshops

Maybe your budget will buy books for your library but won't cover special events, such as an author visit. Think about applying for a grant to fund your next staff, student, or visiting author workshop. Depending on the cost of your dream event, you may need more than one money source.

To host visiting authors, many school districts supplement their budgets with donations—monetary or goods and services—from their PTA or local banks, bakeries, bookstores, hotels, and other businesses. They finance large, expensive events with several donations from various sources. Rarely is there a Daddy Warbucks who will fund an entire workshop. But the local baker may bake you a cake for your author reception and the neighborhood restaurant provide a complimentary dinner. Generous community members might be willing to support a program beneficial to young people.

I hope your creative juices are flowing and that you have the skeleton of a plan in your mind for a grant proposal for your library. From that skeleton of an idea, make an outline and try to put some flesh on the bones of an award-winning grant proposal for your media center.

Getting Started

As you prepare to write your grant proposal, continue to fill in the details of the long-range vision for your media center. Get to the store and buy that little spiral notebook in which you can jot down your ideas as they pop into your brain. As ideas come to you, try to follow the rules of brainstorming by thinking of all the possibilities that you can for your media center. Don't edit your ideas for feasibility, spelling, and correct grammar—just brainstorm. Keep the notebook close at hand. You never know when the flash of a good idea is going to hit you. Good ideas sometimes pop up at the least expected times and places.

As you think of them, add the names of the people you need to talk with and make a list of the field trips and site visits you need to make. Remember, a good idea is at the heart of every successful grant, so don't let one slip by without making a record of it. You can refine and embellish it later.

Leonardo da Vinci kept journals or notebooks beside him. He sketched in them, wrote down ideas as they came to him, and drew diagrams of potential projects and ideas. The way I see it, if Leonardo thought it was a good idea, who am I to criticize it?

Once you have brainstormed a list of several grants you could apply for, begin to refine the ideas you think are the most feasible for now.

Next, you must fill in some of the details of your dream before it can become reality. For example, if you want a color printer for your library, try logging onto a manufacturer's Web site to research what type of printer you should get, how much it costs, and what the specifications for it are. Print out the information you find. Start a document or a spreadsheet on your computer and then record the data about the color printer in it. You have now started the budget section of a grant proposal. You are in business!

Enter a Contest

Contests are a great place to cut your grant-writing teeth. I believe in entering any contests that you can that might provide recognition for your students, staff, school, or media center. Any time you can bring positive recognition to your school and media center, it's a step toward your objective. Winning contests and honors fortifies your credibility with fund sources, and in the process of entering contests, you are learning and practicing the skills of writing a winning entry.

Think Solid, Not Earthshaking

Keep in mind that the idea that you start to embellish for a grant proposal does not have to be earthshaking or profound. You just need a good, solid idea that is going to make a difference in student learning, achievement, or understanding. It is fine to take an idea that you have read about or seen somewhere and modify it for your setting. You don't have to come up with a wholly original idea, just one that you can embellish and modify to fit your library and benefit your students and staff.

Strive for Action, Not Perfection

Remember that your goal is to get started on a simple grant request project, not to write the Pulitzer Prize-winning grant of all time. Use the strategy of taking an action, no matter how small, every day to build your grant-writing momentum. Make a phone call. Explore an Internet site devoted to grants. E-mail a media specialist from a neighboring district and see if he knows about any available grants. Read a technology journal while looking for grant opportunities. Start or revise your resume. Write a paragraph describing your mission for your library. You can revise it later. Don't strive for perfection. Just take action. Do something.

Get the show on the road. The people who get grant money are the people who apply for it. Many people have good ideas for grants, but the only people who will ever get the grants are ones who apply. Don't let fear of failure keep you in the status quo. Get up and boogie! Getting money is a function of persistence and discipline.

Project Objectives

At the same time you are planning these projects, you also need to focus on your objectives. Decide what you want to accomplish with your grant project and then spell out your objectives in a measurable way. Once you have some clear, measurable goals, you will be able to see how your project fits with the goals of your potential benefactor.

Grant proposal writing is a fluid process. While you are writing one proposal, others may be in the idea development stage. Keep in motion; keep the momentum going.

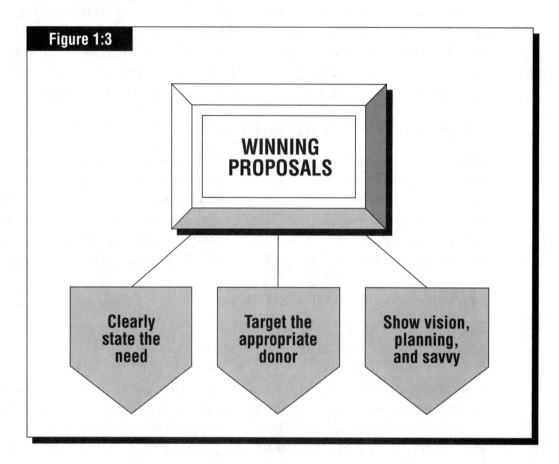

Figure 1:3

WINNING PROPOSALS

Clearly state the need

Target the appropriate donor

Show vision, planning, and savvy

Stop now and get your first few ducks in a row. You've begun to dream your dream and it's time to get started:

■ Start keeping your journal to note ideas to consider, people to interview.

■ Begin your research by visiting other media centers and exploring relevant Web sites.

■ Get others involved by talking with your principal, other administrators, key teachers, and community members.

Chapter 2

Go Where the Grants Are

Research is the act of going up alleys to see if they are blind.

Picture in your mind those specially trained truffle pigs in France. You know, the ones who can sniff out truffles that no one can see buried in the ground? Our goal is to be grant sniffers—extraordinaire! Where shall we start?

There are multiple funding sources waiting to be tapped for our media centers. Our job is to be good detectives and find those sources, and after that to become marketing experts and sell our vision and our need for funding it to the right grantor.

In the world of grant-making, there are private, corporate, and government sources at the local, state, and federal level, and each of them has funds to award. The trick is to make a good match. Let's put you into position to be at the right time and the right place so that we can match you with the ideal grantor. See Appendix B for examples of potential fund sources.

One of your most important jobs as you begin to shop for grant money is to learn about the mission or goals of prospective benefactors. Grant makers have a passionate desire to solve social problems and inequities in society. They want to fund projects that advance their goals.

You also need to learn about prospective benefactors' patterns of giving. Do they award grants in your locale? What kinds of grants have they awarded recently and to whom? What are their application deadlines?

As you prepare to write your grant proposal and market your program to benefactors, keep these questions in mind:

■ What is in it for the funding organization if they fund my grant?

■ What is the organization's mission?

■ Where does the grant maker's vision intersect with my program's goals?

■ How can I market my project to appeal to this entity?

Organize Your Research

Good research practice can help you find funding sources that match the profile of your needs and dreams. Librarians are the best researchers on Earth, so this can be one of the easier tasks you face. You will need to keep good records and be organized as you search for a sponsor. A potential grantor might not fit your current project, but might be a perfect prospect for your next project.

Three-by-five index cards work as well as anything to record your data. I like to use colored index cards to indicate the type of money source—one color for federal agencies, another for private foundations, and a third for community foundations. If you jot the name of the foundation, the address, contact person, information about projects they fund, and Web site address, you can build a colorful file of potential funding sources.

You may prefer to start a spreadsheet or a database and enter your data directly into it. Either way, the important thing is to gather the information and keep track of it in an organized manner for easy retrieval. Whatever method you choose, this file will be a building block in your grant-seeking program. Keep it current.

Some Tips as You Search for Funding Sources

Stay Flexible

It is common for corporate foundations to have unstructured grant application processes. In one way this can make your effort easier because you do not need to write such a formal grant proposal. On the other hand, since the guidelines are not as clear, it can make it more difficult to try to hit the target with your proposal.

Make Contacts

It can be helpful if you know someone in a corporation. Corporations tend to support organizations with which they already have a working relationship. Does your school have a corporate partner? If so, that would be a reasonable organization to explore as you seek a grant sponsor.

If you know someone in a corporation, you might be able to gain some pertinent information. Ask about any potential grant money the company might have and what the goals for spending it are. Begin to build a relationship with potential donors. Learn the phone number and name of the secretary to the person in charge of corporate giving. Add that information to your index card or database for future reference.

Be kind and professional to each person you speak with at the organization. Good manners go a long way. You never know who the informal leaders in an organization are. Your kindness to the executive secretary may be remembered months later when your grant proposal arrives in the mail.

Start Close to Home

Before writing a formal grant proposal to a foundation as you search for funding, you might consider seeking funding from a local corporation or business. Local businesses can be excellent sources for funding in the community. Seeking funding from a local business is an excellent, low-risk way for you to start your fund-raising career.

Do you want to reward your student library volunteers with an end-of-the-year breakfast? Write up your plan and take it to the manager of the grocery store where your school families shop. Asking for orange juice and bagels for 10 students is a great way to start your grant-writing career. If your grocer supports your request, you have your first "grant"—almost painlessly.

At the volunteer breakfast, credit the grocer. Thank her in your parent newsletter and send a copy of the published article with your thank-you note. Make bookmarks for your volunteers with a credit line on them to the grocer and include one of those in your letter. Sing the grocer's praises at the next PTA meeting. Write a letter to the Chamber of Commerce saluting the grocer. Make your grocer feel proud of her generosity. Give credit where credit is due.

Many local and national groups offer funding or prizes for special projects. The Daughters of the American Revolution (DAR) and Sertoma International are two groups in our community who have assisted media specialists.

Types of Grants

Foundations

Various kinds of foundations may have funding available for your media center:

■ *Independent or Private Foundations* frequently fund public television and radio programs; you'll see or hear their names among the credits at the end. There are almost 50,000 private foundations in the United States, many founded by prosperous families who support arts and humanities or other special interests. Researching their interests and grant criteria is important preliminary work for crafting your grant request. A majority of family foundations limit their funding to their local community. There's no sense in applying for funding for your Kansas media center when the foundation funds projects only in Mississippi. You will learn this information in your research. Don't forget to note the foundation's special interests on your index card or in your database.

The Ezra Jack Keats Foundation, for example, offers mini-grants for innovative programs that combat illiteracy in public schools. For information about these grants, contact Executive Director, Ezra Jack Keats Foundation, 450 14th St., Brooklyn, NY 11215.

The Read-in Foundation focuses on libraries, inviting schools around the world to create their own community literacy projects. Visit the Read-in Web site at <www.readin.org> for information on their funding practices.

■ *Company-Sponsored Foundations* usually fund projects relating to the company's interests, often exclusively in the locale or regions where the company operates. Corporate foundations typically fund projects that will enhance the corporate image, provide a benefit to their employees, make the community more valuable to the corporation, or help the company reach corporate goals. Corporate Web sites offer information about these foundations. One of your jobs as you research and plan your project is to figure out how your goals for your media center fit with the company's goals.

For example, 3M offers Professional Development Grants each year. Library recipients are chosen from national applicants. The grants are given to American Library Association's (ALA) New Members Round Table (NMRT) and are called 3M/NMRT Professional Development Grants. Recipients are chosen for their activism in the association, their commitment to librarianship, and their career development goals. For more information about the grants, contact 3M or check out the ALA Web site at <www.ala.org>.

■ *Community Foundations* work with individuals, corporations, and other non-profit organizations to fund projects in the local area. Your city or county may have a community foundation whose mission is congruent with yours.

Government Funds

Many government agencies have grant money they are charged with awarding. The art is to find which agency grants funds for your type of project and then to meet the complex qualifications and guidelines of a government grant. If you are allergic to red tape, don't start your grant-writing career by applying for a government grant. The process is comparable to taking a graduate course. I recommend that you apply to a smaller grantor to start with and get some success at that level before tackling a government grant. When you have the experience of writing a winning grant application or two, you are ready to try for the big bucks of a government grant. I would definitely recommend working with a team if you plan to apply for a government grant because of its complexity and the research and diligence it will require.

The government publishes *The Grant Award Actions Database* for you to access on the Internet at <http://Web99.ed.gov/grant/grtawd00.nsf>. This is a one-stop source of extensive information on all the current year's Education Department (ED) grants.

The following are some of the types of government grants:

■ *Library Services and Construction Act (LSCA)* grants are given to state libraries, earmarked for specific types of library projects. Each state has its own rules and regulations for awarding funds, but they are all governed by the federal legislation. Request the *LSCA Handbook* from your state library for information about the kinds of proposals your state funds. There are many restrictions, so read the regulations carefully.

■ *Library Services and Technology Act (LSTA)* **Special Populations** grants are open to libraries of all types. To learn more about them, send a letter of intent to your state library and request an application and guidelines.

■ *National Endowment for the Humanities (NEH)* was set up by Congress to support research and education projects in the humanities. If you are interested in pursuing NEH funding, be sure to seek assistance at <http://www.neh.fed.us/>. NEH has very high standards. I would consider working with a professor from a local college or university if you are seriously pursuing NEH funding. You may need the research, expertise, and experience of a past recipient to compete in this league. NEH offers a publication entitled *Humanities Projects in Libraries and Archives; Guidelines and Application Instructions*. This document can be ordered from NEH, Division of Public Programs. It is item number OMB #3136-0118.

ALA works in conjunction with NEH on some projects. For more information about ALA's humanities program, see their publications or contact the ALA director of public programs online at <http://www.ala.org/alaorg/staff/staff.html>.

■ *State Humanities Councils* fund a variety of projects. If you are seeking funding for a visiting author or a writer's workshop, this might be a venue for you. You will find a bibliography of state arts and humanities councils in Appendix H of this book.

Resources to Help Find Grantors

Internet Searches

When you use keyword searches for grant money, you will have many hits. Be sure and use basic Boolean search tips.

Another way to research is to search the Internet for specific technology manufacturers' Web sites and look for any foundations they might have established. It is possible to spend hours on the Internet searching for potential grant funds. The harvest of prospective donors is usually huge and will give you hours of data to sift through. Following are some Web sites to try:

- **RightGrant Online** is a free school grant locating service at <www.teachersuniverse.com>.

- **The Foundation Center** is a service organization that helps grant seekers find information about potential donors. Foundation Center libraries are located at several sites around the country and at a Web site, <http://www.fdncenter.org>.

- **The Council on Foundations** at <http://www.cof.org/links> keeps information on independent foundations.

- **Catalog of Federal Domestic Assistance (CFDA)** is a U.S. government publication, both print and online, available from the Superintendent of Documents, Washington, DC 20402 or at <http://www.cfda.gov/>.

- **The Federal Register** is a daily government publication, also available from the Superintendent of Documents, that will keep you posted on federal grant application deadlines, rules, and regulations. Access it online at <http://www.access.gpo.gov/su_docs/aces/aces140.html>.

Directories

Several foundation directories are available at your local community library, the nearby college library, or at one of the Foundation Center libraries. These directories will lead you to foundations, their guidelines, annual reports, contact information, and other pertinent data:

- **Corporate 500: The Directory of Corporate Philanthropy** is a comprehensive directory of funding information published by Public Management Institute, San Francisco, California. ISBN# 0916664580.

- **Corporate Giving Directory** includes sample grant recipients. Taft Group in Detroit, Michigan, publishes it. ISBN# 1569954046.

- **The Foundation Directory**, published in New York by the Foundation Center, is your source for information about some of the largest foundations in the country. ISBN# 087959440.

- **The Foundation Directory, Part 2**, also published by the Foundation Center, has information on mid-sized foundations that make grants from $25,000 to $100,000. ISBN# 0879549459.

- **Foundation Grants to Individuals**, published by the Foundation Center, lists foundations that make grants of $2,000 or more to individuals. ISBN# 0879543876.

- *Statistical Abstract of the United States, 2000: The National Data Book* lists foundations with less than $1 million in assets that make grants of $100,000 or more. It is published in Austin, Texas, by Hoover's Business Press. ISBN# 1573110639.

- *The National Directory of Corporate Giving*, published by the Foundation Center, has excellent information on funding sources. ISBN# 0879548886.

Journal and Newsletter Searching

Start scouring the library and technology journals and newsletters for current grant opportunities. Look for the columns entitled *Grant Awards* and *Grant Deadlines*. Look in *Cable in the Classroom, e-School News, electronic school, Learning and Leading with Technology, Media and Methods, net connect* (supplement to *Library Journal* and *School Library Journal*), *Technology Today*, and other educational technology journals.

You probably already read school library professional journals. Watch carefully for notices of grant opportunities in columns in *American Library, The Book Report, Knowledge Quest, Library Journal, Library Talk, Horn Book, School Library Journal, Voice of Youth Advocates,* and others. Make it your habit to check the journals every month for current grant information. You may see nothing of interest for six months and then hit the jackpot in the seventh month. Keep your eye out for those truffles! Don't lose faith in finding a good match for your needs.

Search Tips

- *Write or call for application forms and guidelines.* A first step in getting started writing a grant proposal to a private foundation is to write or call for the application forms. The addresses for foundations can be found in the reference books mentioned or online if the foundation has a Web site. Once you receive the information, start a file folder for that foundation and file it in your Potential Donors file. You may need an accordion file for the annual reports and the file folders you have established for each foundation. The annual reports are informative but usually hefty. Hanging files will also work well for bulky reports.

- *Contact past grantees.* If you can learn from the foundation or from your research the name of someone who has gotten a grant from this foundation, contact that person and learn more about the grant, the process, and the winning proposal. My experience has been that educators are happy and eager to share their victories with colleagues. There are no better team players on Earth than educators, so make a call and learn from someone else's experience.

- *Build relationships.* Once you have found potential donors, you need to begin to establish relationships with them. A simple act of courtesy, such as clipping the picture of someone you know in the paper who is on the board of the local

DAR, can help you make a connection. Cut the picture out and send it to the board member with a thoughtful note. Begin simply to establish connections. Build a bridge between your program and potential supporters.

There is grant money out there. You can find and claim some for your library. It is well within your reach.

■ *Network.* Sometimes, the fastest and easiest way to find a grantor is to network with your colleagues to learn who has gotten grants from whom. Go fishin'! Ask your neighboring media specialists. Ask the public librarians. Ask your favorite listserv. Ask your sorority or fraternity associates, your professional association, and the staff at the nearby school of library information management. Someone you know knows where there is grant money available and waiting for you. Jot down in your spiral notebook the sources you hear about.

■ *Send a query letter.* When you find a potential grantor, a solid next step is to send a query letter telling about your idea and explaining its merits. This is a little like dangling bait in the water of the grant pool. Make it short, upbeat, and to the point. Describe your plan in one paragraph. Probably you will be inquiring about one of your component dreams, not your big-picture dream, so you can easily describe it in a paragraph.

State the reason for your request and a ballpark figure for the amount of funding you will need. Include a needs statement, the target population, and some statistics. Request a funding application. Be sure to include the grantor's name, title, and address, and direct it to the appropriate person. Also include a brief profile of your school.

If you feel it would be appropriate, request a list of past grantees and reviewers to be included in your packet. If that does not seem appropriate, request general information on the types of reviewers they use—their backgrounds, professions, and criteria on which they are selected. If all the reviewers are educators, it might make a difference in how you write your grant. If you know that some of the reviewers were noneducators, you definitely be more careful about using common education jargon.

Once you have received that information, call a past grantee, if you can. Introduce yourself, explain how you got her name, and ask some questions that may help you as you write your grant proposal.

For example, I contacted a consultant who has worked with several state departments of education. She had good advice for new grant writers: Focus on what you want to fund. Set a well-defined goal. Involve anyone who will be collaborating with you, such as administration, legal counsel, and teachers, from the beginning before you start writing. Be succinct. Tell what you're going to do, how you'll do it, how you'll measure it, and what it will cost.

In that grant proposal writer's opinion, the hardest part about writing grants is first deciding what you want to do and then getting people to buy in to your plan once you've started the process.

This grantee knows what she is talking about. She got a $6.8 million five-year statewide grant on her third try.

■ *Use listservs for school librarians.* A listserv is an electronic conference or electronic discussion group that allows people with similar interests to keep in touch with one another and to follow new developments in their area of interest. See Appendix K for a sample list of listservs.

Listservs are a convenient and economical way to network with others who have the same or similar jobs as yours. You can learn what grants others in your trade have gotten and what tips they may have for you. You can bounce your proposal ideas off colleagues and get their feedback. You can also be a listserv lurker, one who subscribes and reads the postings but doesn't respond. If you are shy, you may find lurking a comfortable way to enter the world of listservs.

■ *Go back to school.* Some colleges and universities offer a traditional 16-week graduate level course in grant writing. If you are seeking additional graduate credits, see if your local college or university offers a grant-writing course. Maybe you can learn more about grant writing and get graduate credit at the same time.

Another educational option is to attend a workshop or seminar in grant writing. There are full- or half-day seminars offered by national presenters. It is also possible to contact a presenter who will design a seminar or workshop in grant writing specifically for your faculty or school district and will conduct it at your location.

A third educational option is to take a Web-based course. Sites such as Grantswriters.com at <http://grantwriters.com/training.htm> offer interactive online courses in grant writing. This is a convenient option for those who live far from a college campus but want to enroll in a course.

■ *Consult journals and print media.* In the bibliography of this book you will find several journals that have regular columns announcing upcoming grant competitions and their submission dates. Many books have been written on grant writing, and each has suggestions for finding potential donors. Be adventurous—try an online journal such as *From Now On: The Educational Technology Journal* at <http://www.fno.org/>.

■ *Search the Web.* It's a great way to find potential funding sources. See the bibliography in this book for some suggestions. You can subscribe to online databases that track grant and foundation funding information. For instance, the *GRANTS Database,* available online through Dialog and through Knowledge Express Data Systems, identifies about 9,000 public and private programs that make grants. Find ordering information online at <http://www.oryxpress.com/order.htm>.

■ *Learn from professional organizations and neighbors.* American Library Association, American Association of School Librarians (AASL), academic fraternities, and other professional associations, such as National Education Association (NEA) and American Society for Curriculum Development (ASCD), have information about funding sources for you. Most of these organizations have Web sites that display information on grant funding opportunities.

Visit media specialists in neighboring schools. Ask questions. See how others are solving the problems with which you are wrestling. Your colleagues can be excellent resources for you.

As you search for potential donors, you will see that you need to modify your dream to fit the requirements of the grant-making entity. Finding potential grant sources is an ongoing endeavor. You need to keep your grant-writing ear to the ground. Finding a benefactor is a little like finding the right job. You want to find an organization whose mission and goals are compatible with your own. Scouring Web sites, directories, and annual reports to learn more about the grant sources is one way to find a match for you and your vision.

■ *Attend conferences.* There are many good ideas at the national AASL conference or your state or regional library conferences. Sessions and presenters can be gold mines of best practices and great ideas. Listen to the presenters. Ask questions. Talk to the vendors. Who has seen projects worth reproducing? Attend the sessions on grant writing and learn from both the presenter and the participants.

Attending a conference devoted solely to grant writing is an excellent option, if you can afford it. Technology groups such as *eSchool News online* sponsor meaningful conferences. *Grants & Funding for School Technology: A Strategic Conference for K–12 School Leaders* is a conference sponsored by *eSchool News online.* For information about it, see their Web site at <http://www.eschoolnews.org/>.

If you live in or near a large city, you'll find many opportunities to attend grant-writing seminars. In Boston, for instance, the Foundation Center sponsors grant-writing workshops. Technical Development Corporation, the Center for Nonprofit Management at Boston Center for Adult Education, and the School of Management and Administrative Services at Lesley College also sponsor workshops in Boston. Make some calls to see if there are similar opportunities in your town.

■ *Collect annual reports.* Log on to a foundation's Web site or write a letter and request an annual report. There is nothing like an annual report to give you the real scoop on a foundation or corporation. You will see how the organization portrays itself and what its priorities are. Reading the annual report helps you know your potential grantor much better.

Highlight language that you may want to include somewhere in your grant proposal. We all love to hear our favorite words and phrases repeated back to us. Reading some of his or her own words in your proposal is sure to impress the prospective donor favorably.

File the annual reports and save them for future projects. While the grant you are seeking right now may not involve technology, your next one might. Hang on to that IBM annual report.

■ *Cultivate a state ally.* Personnel at the state department of education and at the state library are good contacts. Call people at those agencies and describe to them the plan for which you are seeking funding. See if they know where there might be funding for your project. They can give you feedback, cheer you on, point you in another direction, give you good advice, and even call you when a new request for proposal (RFP) comes through that sounds like a match to your project. Your state library contact might even be willing to collaborate with you in writing a grant proposal.

While you have a state department of education person on the phone line, ask him to refer you to a past recipient of a grant of the type you are seeking. Give that recipient a call and ask for guidance, suggestions, or advice.

If your proposal is intriguing and you have visited with the proper people at the state level, you may be asked to submit a full proposal. But remember, just because you were encouraged to submit a proposal doesn't mean your grant will be funded. There are miles to go before you achieve that goal.

If you are asked to submit a full proposal, stay in touch with your state contact. Don't be pushy, but your contact might be willing to read your final draft before you submit it and give you tips. As you progress in writing the sections of your grant, check in with your contact when you have questions.

Start Your Search Close to Home

Start close to home and find out as much as you can about potential fund sources. Find an up-to-date directory of foundations for your area or state. Seek help from the librarian at your local library to find a foundation directory. Think about planning a field trip to the nearest Foundation Center Library. If that is not possible, check out the Foundation Center's Web site at <http://fdncenter.org/onlib/index.html> to learn the site nearest to you.

Be sure to use current reference materials as you shop for foundations and grant-givers. Beware outdated directories. You could spin your wheels pursuing funding from a defunct foundation or one that no longer offers grants.

Knowing someone on the board of a local foundation or corporation is also helpful as you begin your grant-writing career. If you have a contact within the offices of a potential donor, find out what you can about the kinds of projects for which the organization typically awards grants. Seek guidance from those in the know. Remember, you are not looking for insider trading information, just helpful tips for finding a potential grant source and writing a winning grant proposal. Ask if you may see a copy of a project that was funded last year. You don't know until you ask, but be sure not to make a nuisance of yourself. Many foundation offices are run on a shoestring and often manned with volunteer help only.

At this point in your project you should

- Organize your research.
- Consider the type of grant you wish to seek—federal, private, or other.
- Explore your search resources such as the Internet, directories, special libraries, and journals.
- Write or call for forms and guidelines.
- Connect with potential grantors.
- Send a query letter.
- Join a listserv.
- Take a grant proposal writing class.
- Attend a conference.
- Order annual reports.

ad Grants nd Form a Writing Team

Two dogs will kill a lion.

—Hebrew Proverb

Make it a high priority to become a grant reader. It's one of the best ways to learn to write winning grant proposals. If your school district or parish is lucky enough to have support from a foundation, volunteer to be on the team that reads grant applications. The group of readers will probably be small, friendly, and eager to help you learn to sort the worthy from the unsuccessful grant proposals.

Do you know someone who reviews grants? If so, call and ask questions:

■ How did you get started reading grants?

■ Do you review grant proposals by mail or in meetings with other panelists?

■ Can you describe some of the scoring systems you have used?

■ Would you be willing to give me feedback on my grant proposal when it's written?

■ What mistakes do you typically encounter in the proposals you read?

■ How much time do you devote to proposal reading and how many proposals do you normally read per grant?

Send your resume or curriculum vita with a cover letter to organizations expressing interest in having you review grants for them. Highlight your credentials in your letter to the chair of the review committee. See Appendix G for a sample resume. (It's a real one. Librarian and consultant Carolyn Hoffman graciously shared hers with us.)

Contest Judge

Another possible forum for you is to volunteer to serve on the committees who select contest winners. Typically your state or local professional organization recognizes outstanding media specialists. Volunteer to serve on that state committee. Volunteer to be on the scholarship committee for the American Library Association at <http://www.ala.org>, for the American Association of School Librarians <http://www.ala.org/aasl/>, or for the International Reading Association at <http://www.reading.org/>.

Watch for the "Call for Nominations: Council, Committee Applications Available" column in *American Libraries*. The columnist recommends that your letter of application or nomination include professional qualifications and the name of the committee for which you are volunteering or nominating someone.

Some library vendors sponsor contests to honor librarians. Contact Follett, Grolier's, or another library product vendor who sponsors contests.

If you are chosen to sit on a selection committee, you will gain insight into how others market themselves and what attributes the grantors are seeking. You'll learn some "do's" and "don'ts" of proposal writing. You'll learn insider tips on what wins points and friends and what turns the judges off. The "don'ts" are just as important as the "do's" when you are learning marketing strategies for your media center and yourself.

Believe it or not, serving on the committees who read those applications will hone your skills for writing and for identifying a winning proposal. You will see applications that are concise, colorful, and congruent with the goals of the contest. Transfer those skills to writing grant proposals and you will be in the winners' circle soon.

Reviewing Grants

When you are invited to review grants, you will be asked to follow the review criteria of the funding organization. You will be asked to evaluate the strength and scope of the proposal; the credentials, past history, and credibility of the personnel who will be implementing the grant; the accuracy and thoroughness of the budget; and the overall impact of the proposed project.

You will be asked to write meaningful comments on each of the requests you read. The grantor will read these and may share, with the proposal writer upon request. So be specific, meaningful, fair, and grammatically correct. Do not depend on spell-checker for correct spelling; keep your dictionary handy and use it.

When you volunteer to review grant proposals, you learn to use the grantor's review criteria or scoring rubric. Each funding entity and each grant competition may have its own set of criteria. In general, you will find that a specified number of points are possible in each section of the proposal. We will look at each of those sections in depth in a later chapter.

Local Foundations

If you have foundations in your community, give one of them a call and volunteer to read grant proposals for them. Even if they are not affiliated in any way with school library media centers, the experience will still help you by familiarizing you with the format of a grant proposal and the qualities that make for a winning proposal. It doesn't matter, as you are learning to write proposals, whether the ones you are reading are education-related or not. The formats will be similar, as will be the critical attributes of winning proposals.

Many school districts have education foundations that support them. If your school district is interested in enlisting outside support for innovative projects, think about forming an educational foundation. It is a relatively simple process to form a foundation, and the rewards are high. For an article on forming educational foundations, go to <http://www.fno.org/fnosept91.html>.

Foundations formed specifically to support innovation in school districts are prime examples of potential grantors for media specialists. A school librarian who designs a project and writes a winning proposal to fund it can have a wide impact on the students, school, and community.

For an example of a foundation established to support the Shawnee Mission Kansas School District, see Appendix J. There you will see a brochure soliciting grant proposals for the Shawnee Mission Education Foundation. Visit them online at <http://www.smef.org> to gain an idea of the type of grant competitions organized by education foundations.

State Grants

Your state department of education probably uses grant-reading teams to select recipients of state grants. Contact the person who assembles teams to read grants, and volunteer. Send your curriculum vita with a letter stating your interest. Don't be disappointed if you are not selected on your first try, but continue to volunteer until you are chosen to read. Also, let your boss know you'd like to be on a proposal-reading team. He may be able to recommend you.

When you are selected to serve on a proposal review team, you will be asked to take a pledge of confidentiality, a critical value in proposal review. (I never tell anyone but my supervisor that I am serving on a grant review team.)

Once chosen to read grants, you'll typically be mailed 10 to 20 grant proposals to read by a certain date, along with a scoring rubric and specific directions for reading, scoring, and commenting on the proposals. It will take you an hour or two to read each of the state grant proposals, then more time to comment on and score them. The good news is that you usually have a week or two to get your assignment done. As you know, people spend countless hours writing grant proposals. They deserve to have careful, committed, unbiased readers review them—in confidence.

You may also be asked to read grants online. You will be assigned a user name and password to a Web site where you can log on to read and score the proposals assigned to you.

Either way, after reading, scoring, and commenting on your assigned proposals, you will probably be asked to drive to the state department of education offices to meet with the panel who have read the same proposals. After an orientation session, you will meet in small groups and discuss the proposals you have read and scored. You will be asked to justify your scores, compare them to the other panelists, and listen to the others' perspectives. You will see how your scoring compares with theirs, which projects will receive funding, and which won't.

These state grant review events can last a half-day, a full day, even two or more days. Your expenses will be paid and you may even receive an honorarium.

Federal Grants

Once you have cut your grant-reading teeth on local and state grant proposals, it may be time to volunteer to read federal grant proposals. Reading federal grant proposals gives you an excellent idea of what is required in submitting one. The federal government needs qualified volunteers to read grant proposals for several programs. One of these is the U.S. Department of Education, Office of Postsecondary Education, Teacher Quality Enhancement Grant Program. This office is usually seeking new, qualified field reader candidates. When you contact them, they will ask you for a two-page resume and a cover letter requesting inclusion in the Higher Education Field Reader System registry. Information on Higher Education Programs (HEP) can be found at <http://www.ed.gov/office/OPE/HEP>.

Several areas in the Department of Education use grant readers. Before you volunteer, check out the Web site or make some calls to see where your interests lie and where your background would make the best fit.

Reading federal grant proposals is grueling work, not a pastime for those with low energy or who prefer a slow pace and lower expectations. Typically, if you are selected to read federal grant proposals, you will be asked to travel to Washington, D.C., where you will meet in a hotel with a large group of proposal readers and alternates. You will be given orientation, be assigned to a team of six to eight readers, and be expected to follow a rigorous schedule of reading, scoring, and discussion.

Federal grant proposals are long and complex, and the scoring rubrics are intricate. Readers must provide written comments for each section, carefully based on the scoring rubrics. The days you spend reading grant proposals are long and lonely; you may find yourself locked in your hotel room reading and writing for days on end. Writer's cramp is an occupational hazard. The pressure is tight to get your daily assignment of grant proposals read, scored, discussed, and approved. It is not uncommon for several new proposal readers to drop out because of stress as the week in Washington progresses. That is why alternates are appointed for each federal grant review project.

When you read federal grant proposals, you will find yourself running with the big dogs. I believe it is worth the effort that you give, however. You will quickly learn what makes a fundable proposal and gain insight into the scope of a federal grant-writing project. Plus, you are being a good citizen when you volunteer to review grant proposals; you are serving as a steward of the taxpayers' dollars.

You begin to see that applying for a federal grant really is within your capabilities. You need a solid idea, a strong proposal-writing team, a gung-ho collaborating partner or institution, and some time to work on the proposal. You can do it.

A Grant Proposal Reader's Responsibilities

As a proposal reviewer, you will be expected to

- Give specific written feedback for each application.
- Provide helpful written suggestions to the writer.
- Review the grant proposals objectively, without bias or personal feelings.
- Join in the discussion when the review team meets together.
- Keep all information confidential.
- Identify any conflict of interest.
- Document your critique and provide a rationale.
- Use tact and discretion.

In addition, practiced grant proposal readers offer these tips:

- Take notes while reading.
- Read quickly and with purpose.
- Focus on the information related to the scoring rubric.
- Look for key words and phrases.
- Have a calculator nearby.

Learn from Reading Grant Proposals

You will probably find that your performance as a grant reader, as well as writer, will improve with experience. You will begin to see some of the more common mistakes grant writers make, such as failure to follow directions, unclear writing, and nonspecific or inaccurate budgets.

Another common error you may encounter is the proposal writer's assuming too much prior information on the part of the reader. In their familiarity with their school, its programs, and its community, writers sometimes forget that the proposal reader likely knows nothing about their schools or communities, nor what either the writer or the students are like. The reader may be totally unfamiliar with the content of the proposal. As you read and score grant proposals, you will begin to see how some writers have a knack for describing their populations, defining their projects succinctly, and presenting a compelling need for the project.

After performing this proposal-reading service for others, you will gain confidence in your ability to write winning grant proposals. You will also become a more valuable resource to your school community because you will learn what grant money is available and how to access it.

Be sure that your principal and superintendent are aware if you are given the honor of reading grant proposals. When you look good, they look good. It is good for your school and your district when you are selected to review grant proposals. It's an experience you can add to your resume.

Internal Review Team

Some organizations that write and submit grant proposals on a regular basis organize internal review teams. They write the grant proposal well in advance of the submission deadline and then have their own team evaluate their proposal against the proposal guidelines and scoring rubric, revising to reflect the internal feedback. By the time the grant is submitted, the kinks are probably out of it.

There is nothing to prevent you, your library clerk, and a volunteer or two from performing the same analysis on your proposals. These folks care as much as you do and have everything to gain for their efforts. Be objective. Step back and take an unbiased look. Where do you need more supporting details? Where are you redundant? Where are you understating the case? We will talk more about revising your work in Chapter 7.

Build a Grant-Writing Team

The easiest way for most people to apply for a grant is as a member of a team. Assembling an eager team to help you write your proposal and working together to accomplish your goals can be rewarding. You strengthen your own role as the idea person when you include others' ideas in your proposal. More participants may also broaden your project's appeal to your potential grantor.

Cooperative learning, an effective strategy in the classroom, is equally effective in seeking grants. Having assigned roles makes the task easier and the process smoother for all.

As you assemble a grant writing team, consider including some variation of the following roles. You may find yourself and your colleagues playing more than one role. Consider seeking potential team members from a library listserv, from among friends and colleagues at neighboring schools or library school, or family members.

- *Reader.* The person in this critical position reads the request for proposal (RFP) carefully, highlighting vital information such as the date the proposal is due, maximum length, type size and font, and spacing required. The reader could be you, your spouse, the school secretary, a library aide, or a clerk.

- *Abstract Writer.* This person can see the big picture of your grant proposal and describe it accurately and compactly in one powerful page. Write the abstract yourself, if succinct, expository writing is your forte. If not, get a friend, a colleague, or your boss to write this one-page summary of your project.

- *Number Cruncher.* You will need an accountant type on your team to calculate the budget you'll need, adjust it as you revise your proposal, and check that it meets all the criteria specified in the RFP. You will need a budget narrative, a written description of the budget, and a detailed budget-at-a-glance. Each reference to costs in your proposal needs to match budget figures. The budget needs to include nitty-gritty details—when stipends are paid, cost of salaries, Federal Insurance Contributions Act (FICA) deductions, and other benefits.

- *Researcher.* You will probably be required to cite research that supports your project. The researcher will search the Internet and Educational Resources Information Center (ERIC) as well as academic journals for research that supports your proposal. Literature searches can be time-consuming, but worth it when your findings persuade the grantor to fund your project.

- *Statistician.* Many organizations make grants only to entities that meet certain race, gender, ethnic, and socioeconomic criteria. The statistician needs to have the perseverance to dig through the archives, ferret out the data required by the RFP, confirm their accuracy, and make sure that you have translated the data correctly to the grant proposal. Treasure these statistics, file them in a safe place, and update them as you receive updated information each year, for almost every grant you may apply for will require you to furnish this information.

- *Shopper.* The shopper must be willing to research costs, brands, consultants, and other factors that bear on the source and cost of items and services for which you are requesting funding. What kind of laptop computer, with which accessories, costs how much? Do you need a consultant? What will the consultant cost per day? The success of your application will depend in part on the accuracy of this information. If the grant you seek is for a laptop for your library and you underestimate the cost, you're not likely to get the grant.

■ *Proofreader.* This person needs to be a whiz at spotting a misused or misspelled word or a grammatical error. She must read and reread the grant proposal from the title page to the last appendix to make sure it is grammatically and syntactically correct. Who proofreads your school newsletter or staff bulletin? Could he help you? Were you an English teacher in a past life? You may have the necessary credentials. You may feel irritated when the proofreader finds a juicy error, but treat her kindly, for you need her.

■ *Veteran.* Every proposal-writing team needs a veteran who has written successful proposals. This guru will give you tips as you write and keep you motivated with tales of treasure at the end of the grant-proposal rainbow. Your principal, library coordinator, or next-door teacher may fill the bill. Educators are usually eager to assist one another.

■ *Editor.* Someone needs to assemble the component sections into one coherent document. Look for a person who's a whiz at word processing and a master of consistent, coherent writing. The editor makes the team-written proposal speak with one voice; ensures that headings, type faces and sizes, and other format considerations conform to the RFP stipulations; and that headings match the wording in the table of contents.

Has the superintendent of schools signed in the required spot? Are the attachments secured to the document or are they still in a stack of papers beside your computer? The editor looks after these details while putting together the final grant proposal.

■ *Key Communicator.* This person's job is to keep the boss in the loop. He reports to the central office intermittently to ensure that the proposal is in sync with school board policy, state purchasing guidelines, and the like, and makes sure that all staff members potentially affected by the grant understand their roles and are amenable to the plan.

■ *Delivery Person.* Somebody has to make sure the precious cargo of your grant proposal gets where it is going. The fine print in the RFP will tell you how and where the document must be delivered. This responsible citizen makes sure the grant proposal is delivered on time in the proper container to the right recipient.

■ *Copy Maker.* Everyone who participated in writing the proposal, as well as those who will have a role in the project if it is funded, will need a copy of the final product. The business office will also need a copy if you will be making purchases through the school district's purchasing department. Your boss needs a copy, and you need a copy for your file. If the document is on the hard drive of your computer, be sure you have a clean copy on a disk, too.

■ *Pace Keeper.* Completing your proposal means keeping on schedule. Once you know the due date for the grant proposal, you can work backwards to establish interim due dates. Weekly meetings keep your team motivated without overwhelming them, though you may need to meet daily as you near completion.

Rarely will you have the luxury of this many people on your grant-writing team. You'll probably have to wear several of the hats yourself. The hours for grant writers are long and pay is poor, so serve coffee and maybe even food at your meetings. Make sure that your own company is good.

Find out if your school district has a grant-proposal writer on staff. Many do, some full-time, others in addition to other duties. If you are fortunate to have such a person in your district, call and make an appointment to see her. Show her your plan and ask for her help. If she cannot help you with the actual writing, will she give you feedback and coach you as you write the proposal?

Meet with Your Team

Once you have formed a team, schedule a planning meeting. You have several tasks to do and many questions to answer. You will want to

■ Establish the goals of your project.

■ Define a time line.

■ Refine the goals of the grant writing team positions.

■ Schedule your next meeting.

■ Set group norms.

Prior to the meeting, make enough copies of the RFP or grant application guidelines so that each person can have one. Highlight the sections of the application that give pertinent specifications, instructions, and pointers for sections. More specific suggestions for highlighting will be given later (Chapter 4).

Brainstorm an outline for your project. If you've already established the parameters and design of your project, see how they fit with the proposal specifications.

Decide which partnerships and alliances, if any, you want to collaborate with on the project—perhaps another school library in your district, in another school district, or even in a private school. You may want to team with a state entity, a public library, or a private company, such as a software vendor.

As a team, decide who will do which tasks:

■ Set your meeting schedules.

■ Organize the agendas for the meetings.

■ Establish internal deadlines.

■ Agree on document format.

The whole is greater than the sum of its parts. Your grant proposal has a much higher probability of success when you write it with a gung-ho team of experts.

Grant-Writing Process

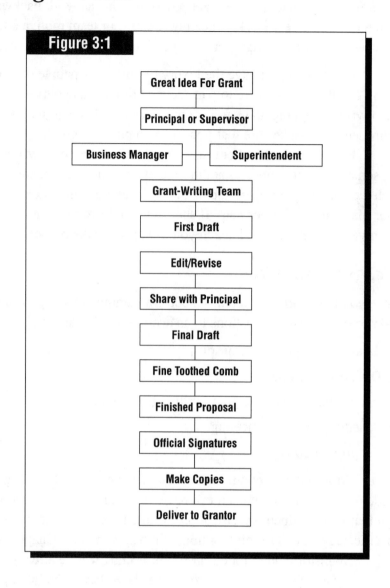

Figure 3:1

- Great Idea For Grant
- Principal or Supervisor
- Business Manager — Superintendent
- Grant-Writing Team
- First Draft
- Edit/Revise
- Share with Principal
- Final Draft
- Fine Toothed Comb
- Finished Proposal
- Official Signatures
- Make Copies
- Deliver to Grantor

Let's review the tasks you may wish to assign yourself at this point in your project:

■ Research ways to become a grant proposal reader.

■ Volunteer to be a contest judge.

■ Explore education and other local foundations.

■ Volunteer to read state and or federal grant proposals.

■ Begin to form a grant writing team.

■ Meet with the team to set goals and establish a schedule for your project.

Chapter 4

Read the Fine Print

In the long run, men hit only what they aim at.

—Henry David Thoreau

In many projects I have the very bad habit of reading the directions only when all else fails. This habit and the act of writing a successful grant are at complete odds. I have had to mend my ways in the department of reading directions. I guarantee you that it is absolutely critical in grant-seeking to scrutinize the entire application.

First Reading

Make yourself a copy of the RFP and sit down with it and a highlighter pen. Each time you see a specific direction, highlight it, for example,

- Date the grant is due,
- Size of print and type of font,
- Formatting rules,
- Spacing requirements,
- Maximum length of abstract, sections, entire document,

- Required attachments,
- Budget restrictions,
- Required signatures,
- Points possible for each section,
- Funding priorities,
- Mailing address,
- Number of copies to submit,
- Application deadline,
- Special requirements or restrictions, including
  collaboration,
  letters of commitment or support,
  statistical data, and
  resumes, and whether
- Appendix allowed.

When you have thoroughly highlighted each section of the proposal, begin reading it again. It takes several reads before the gist of a complicated proposal request becomes clear. There are so many details and directions that one reading may turn you off grant writing forever. Stick with it.

Second and Third Readings

On your second reading, watch for and highlight in a second color any buzzwords the prospective grantor seems to like, so that you have your important instructions in one color and colorful language in another. If the grantor wants proposals to serve the "have-nots in the digital divide," highlight that phrase and plan to include it in your proposal. Highlight any powerful or distinctive words or phrases your target audience seems to favor, and be sure to employ them in your proposal.

Pay close attention to the points each of the sections is worth. Obviously, you will want to spend your greatest energy where you can score the most points.

Read carefully to learn how your project fits the donor's priorities. Find out what the philanthropy will and will not fund. Read between the lines for hints that will help you recognize what might persuade this organization to underwrite your program.

Reading the fine print is a key step in writing a winning grant. On your third reading, use a third color of highlighter to mark any examples of successful proposals that the grantor has included.

Make Copies

Once you've highlighted the nitty-gritty directions and power language, make copies for your grant writing team and highlight each copy. While this may seem like a time-consuming effort, you will be thankful later. You are really learning the donor's rules and regulations as you read and reread the application. Your writer's eye is learning more about this person or organization each time you reread it.

The more you understand this benefactor's priorities, the more likely it is you will write a winning grant proposal. The grantor will not change funding priorities just because you have written such an excellent proposal, especially if it is for a project outside his priorities. He is looking for a perfect match. Read to learn what his priorities are and how you can make them yours.

One thing you may learn from reading the RFP is that the application deadline is so close that you do not have time to put an appropriate proposal together. If that is the case, don't despair. If this grant is an annual event, you and your team may decide that you want to begin work now on a proposal to submit next year.

Getting Ready to Write

As you prepare to write a draft of your grant proposal you will need to stock up on

- Paper,
- Pencils,
- Pens,
- Highlighters,
- Grammar reference book,
- Thesaurus,
- Dictionary, and
- Style manual.

Make sure you have access to a computer, printer, and photocopier. Even before meeting with your grant-writing team, you can start a document in your computer word processing software. Identify and label each section of the proposal and the subheadings under them. Type in "Date due" and "Team member" under each heading. Then when you meet with your grant-writing team, you can agree on the interim due dates and pencil them in on the copies of the document sections you have typed and copied for the team meetings. As team members volunteer to contribute to a section, you will pencil their names in at your team meeting.

If there are subheadings within sections, type those in your document outline.

```
Abstract


Date due_____


Team member_____


(1 page)

(Include project needs, goals, plan,
budget amount, evaluation)
```

Save as You Go

Save your grant proposal on a disk as you work and again once it is complete. That way you can edit, revise, rewrite, and resubmit it for future competitions. You will find that a proposal can be resubmitted several times to different donors with just a little revision. If you do resubmit a proposal with revisions, be meticulously careful to change all pertinent information. Readers are turned off by careless references to another proposal.

Call for Clarification

Don't be afraid to call the grantor. Now is the time to call the program officer if there is something in the RFP that you do not understand or something for which you need clarification. When you call, you may also learn recent information that was not included in the RFP.

Be ready to take notes. Listen carefully and use your best telephone manners. When you briefly describe your project, does it sound like it fits with the priorities of the sponsor? Make a list of your questions before you call so that you don't waste a minute of the officer's time:

- How much money will be spent on the new projects they will be funding?
- How many applications for that money do they anticipate?
- What common errors do applicants make?
- Are their grants ever renewable?
- What would they like to see in a proposal?
- Do they ever review drafts of a proposal and give feedback before the proposal is formally submitted?
- Can they give you a copy of a previously funded proposal that you could read?
- Is it possible for you to have a copy of the reviewer's scoring form?
- Will the organization be offering an RFP workshop? If so, where and when will that be?

If there is a workshop, attend. You can collaborate with others seeking the same funds, meet the sponsor, and learn more about the competition. Don't miss an opportunity like this.

Assess Your Proposal

Ask someone outside of your field to read your proposal. Do you have a sibling who is not in education who would be willing to evaluate it? Find a sharp-eyed but kind reader who is not a school librarian. Give him a copy of your proposal and ask him to note any questions or comments he has. If he can't tell you, in just a few words, what your proposal's mission is, how it will be accomplished, and why it is significant, then you clearly can't expect to win a grant. It is time to revise and rewrite to strengthen and clarify your proposal.

Read Some Winning Grant Proposals

Read some winning grant proposals before you sit down to put cursor to screen to write your own. You wouldn't expect to perform a swan dive on your first try without first watching many good examples. Don't expect to win a grant without reading several winning entries first.

Winning grant proposals are available for reading on the Internet. You will find some at the U.S. Department of Education Web site, <http://www.ed.gov>. Just as you would not want to score student writing before reading samples scored by experts, don't try to write a grant proposal without first reading several winning examples.

Proposal Letter

Some donors prefer to receive a proposal letter before or in place of a formal proposal. A proposal letter is a short grant proposal, usually two to four pages long, written in letter form. The letter explains, in a concise and compelling manner, what you intend to accomplish. A proposal letter is sometimes called a concept paper. With some private donors, a compelling proposal letter is all that is needed to secure a grant. Others use the proposal letter as a way to screen prospective grantees.

Multiple Submissions

Some grant seekers prefer to submit their proposals to several funding sources at the same time. If you choose to make multiple submissions, be sure that you let each recipient know that you are submitting the proposal to other funding sources. There are pros and cons to multiple submissions. All your eggs are not in one basket. You are casting your potential funding net in a broad area.

Cons to making multiple submissions would be that you are using a shotgun versus a rifle approach. Can you find a benefactor whose mission is a perfect match to yours? If so, aim at that one target. If not, consider shopping your proposal around.

If you wait for perfect conditions, you will never get anything done. Keep that thought in mind and get started on your project. Where are you on your "to do" list? Have you

- Read the application several times?

- Made copies and highlighted critical information?

- Gathered the necessary office supplies and equipment?

- Started a draft document on your computer?

- Called the program officer?

- Found another reader to evaluate your proposal?

- Read several examples of funded grant proposals?

- Written a proposal letter?

If so, you are well on your way to success.

Chapter 5

Parts of the Proposal

Writing is the hardest way of earning a living, with the possible exception of wrestling alligators.

—**Olin Miller**

In order to take some of the mystery out of writing a grant proposal, let's define the parts of the proposal. Note that the application or RFP for competitive grant proposals usually states the number of points possible for each section. It is critical for you to match your effort in the development of each of the grant sections to the number of points you can gain.

As a rule of thumb, if there is a page limit to your finished proposal, and there usually is, you should allot yourself a number of pages for each section proportionate to the percentage of points for that section. If the proposal is limited to 10 pages, and 100 points are possible, then you can figure that if the Plan of Action is worth 30 points, you should allot three pages to that section.

For your proposal to stand out from the rest, it needs to offer a distinctive and innovative solution for a defined problem, written in a compelling manner.

Cover Letter

Sometimes you are allowed a cover letter for your proposal, sometimes not. If you do include a cover letter, make sure it presents a clear picture of the problem, the proposed solution, and the anticipated outcomes. It should be one or two pages long, no longer. As you describe the project, tell the reader the anticipated cost and the expected results without repeating all the information in the formal proposal. The cover letter should set the stage and make the reader want to get to the actual proposal.

Your letter should be concise and well written. It should include a synopsis of your budget and briefly introduce the personnel involved. Tell how your proposal will further the grantor's mission and give the reviewer an incentive to read your proposal carefully. The best plan is to write the cover letter last and make it persuasive. View it as the appetizer to a full-course dinner.

Title Page

The title page features the project title and the name of the applicant organization. The grant guidelines will give specific directions regarding what can and cannot be on the title page. Follow them carefully. Writing the title page first can give you a great sense of accomplishment; now you have one section down, just a few more to write.

Unless the RFP directs otherwise, on the title page provide your project title, your library's name, and the name of the funding source to which you are applying. Center this information about one-third down the page. In the lower

Figure 5:1

Gather Round

A Storytelling Workshop Proposal

Blue Skies School Library
Application to Gotrocks Foundation

Ima Goodlibrarian
1234 Storybook Lane
888.987.6543
Date

right-hand corner, include your name, address, phone number, and the date. If you are applying for funds for your school library, include the name of your school, the school address and phone number, and the name of your school district.

Table of Contents

If your proposal is five or more pages long and the application allows it, include a table of contents. The table of contents page should follow the title page and list the page numbers of the major sections and all of the appendixes.

Abstract, Project Summary, or Executive Summary

Sometimes this section is called the **executive summary**. Like a newspaper lead, it includes the **who**, **what**, **where**, **when** and **why** of your project. The abstract is a brief, clear, and concise summary of your proposed project. It is a one-page snapshot of how much money you need, what you want it for, and how it will change the lives of your students—in about 250 words. The abstract section must be short, powerful, and cause the reader to want to read on. What is the problem and how are you going to solve it?

As a challenge, see if you can summarize your whole proposal in one sentence that says who you are, your claim to fame, what you want the grantor to do for you, your budget request, and the major benefits your project will have. Include your project title in the abstract or project summary. If you are successful, your benefactor may use this section for public relations purposes.

If space permits, include background information about your community and your school. If you have special credentials that make you well qualified to manage this project, include them—awards you have won, outstanding accomplishments, previous grant proposals, or other evidence of your unique qualifications to manage this project. If there is not space in this section, your credentials will fit well in the personnel section.

The grantor does not want to hear how our jobs will be made easier, but instead how the lives and skills of students will improve. The grantor wants to know what there is about your proposal that fits perfectly with his mission.

Statement of Need

This section states the problem—what needs to be fixed or improved in your program, library, or school. Focus on the needs of others—students, teachers, parents, local community. Paint a picture of the situation you hope to improve, cite research that supports the need and the proposed solution, and then tie your program back to school, district, state, and national goals.

Keep the sponsor's values in mind as you describe your needs. How can funding your project help the sponsor meet its institutional goals? How can you convince the funding agency that your effort and expertise, coupled with a specific process, technique, program, or curricular change, will remove a barrier or solve the problem you are highlighting?

If you have performed some type of needs assessment that led you to make a long-range plan and seek grant funds, include a summary of that data in your statement of needs. Powerful data, presented well, will make your case convincing.

Most grants require demographic data. Find statistics from your school, district, and community that support your claim of need for the project you propose. Tell your potential benefactor why this project is necessary. Again, tie your project to your school, state, and national goals.

Cite relevant statistics to help you make your case. Use graphs. But don't overload the reader with too many or irrelevant statistics. Find support in the literature for the project you are proposing. An ERIC search can be helpful. Log on to ERIC at <http://www.searcheric.org/>. Search your topic on the Internet for more sources. Are there national or local task force reports that support your plan?

Use comments from local newspaper articles or from teachers or students that support the perceived need for your project. Beware of using phrases like "little is known about . . . ," "no research has been done on . . . ," or "there is no information about . . . " Do your best to find some evidence to support the need for your particular plan.

Make your needs statement specific, not so broad and general that you are describing the woes of the world in general. If you are asking for backpacks for students to carry home library books so their parents can read aloud to them, outline your school's reading comprehension scores. Find journal or published research articles that support the merit of reading aloud to children.

Don't present the case that your students need a computer lab. The case you want to present is that your students need to acquire information retrieval and evaluation skills. That is the need that is causing you to seek a computer lab and the appropriate online databases for them. If you find yourself presenting a case for needing "things," you have not yet refined your needs far enough. State your needs in terms of student outcomes, not equipment.

While your needs statement must be factual and include evidence, try also to put a genuine emotional spin on it. Cite an example of a real-life situation that will be improved if your project is funded. If your students' needs are urgent, work that into your statement. Be sure your benefactor is clear on why your project will be a good investment.

It's a rare grantor that is interested in your personal needs or comfort. Even though your project may improve your working conditions or efficiency, that would not be a compelling argument for the grant. The successful proposal will focus on others, not on self.

Goals and Objectives

In this section of your proposal, explain how your project will address the needs that you described in the previous section. List the goals and objectives that will be accomplished if your project is funded. Focus on academic values.

The goals should clearly state the end result of the project. Goals are an aim or a purpose. You will want a maximum of two or three goals for your project, no more. Don't try to do too much in one grant.

Describe which population, such as students or teachers, will receive what services. State the goals in terms of staff and student needs, not your own. A goal should be a sentence, not a paragraph. The project goals should be concise and overarching. Consider listing your goals in order of importance.

Objectives explain what is going to be done, when and how it is going to be done. Students, teachers, or parents will acquire or refine which skills? Objectives must be measurable and specific and may include strategies. Objectives must be directly related to the evaluation of your project. Objectives must be measurable. Example: By May 2005, 85 percent of the students in the school district in grade three will score at the 75th percentile on the Reference Materials section of the Iowa Test of Basic Skills.

Don't confuse your objectives with your methods. The objectives are the ends and methods are the means. Goals are the long-range, broad statements of your vision. The objectives are the short, specific, measurable plans to achieve the long-range goals. The objectives will provide solutions to the needs outlined earlier in your proposal. The goals should be reasonable and achievable.

Don't forget that it is critical to align your project's goals and objectives with the grantor's. For instance, if you were writing a Goals 2000 grant proposal, you would choose one or two of the Goals 2000 goal statements upon which to base your project. If the proposal you are writing is directed to the SUMI Literacy Foundation, you will want to focus on literacy goals.

Clearly hook your goals and objectives to your school or library's mission statement. Be positive in your writing; be sure to mention if your project is addressing a need not being addressed by any other project.

Your project will probably begin with a set of objectives and end with the accomplishment of these broad goals. What will be the benchmarks of your program's success? Your objectives state what you intend to change and what benchmarks you plan to use to demonstrate success. Your objectives are tied directly to the evaluation of your program.

Plan of Action

Now is the time to let your inner journalist take over. **What** are you planning to do? **Who** will be providing services to whom? **How** much will it cost and how will the money be spent? **When** and **where** will this happen?

The plan of action is a capsule summary of how the planned project will be implemented. Sometimes this section is called the **project description**.

This section tells the details of how you will achieve your goals. In your final draft, you must be organized, sequential, and succinct. Describe your planned actions on a specific timeline. If staff are being trained, include the training schedule. Specify clearly what you plan to do.

Your plan of action must be engaging and innovative to be funded. In today's educational climate, your plan should include problem-based learning and your students should be deeply engaged in learning. In order to appeal to benefactors and to be current, your activities could address

■ Research-based instructional strategies,

■ Innovative curriculum,

■ Staff development plans,

■ Parental involvement,

■ Collaborations with other entities,

■ Focus on national, state, and local standards,

■ Academic achievement,

■ Authentic assessment,

■ Multiple learning modalities, and

■ Family literacy.

In your plan, make your use of technology fresh and innovative and be sure that it is well integrated in the learning process. Keep the focus on the students and the impact that the project will have on them. Whenever possible, include staff development in your plan.

Consider describing

■ Where your project will take place,

■ Methods you will use,

■ Stages of the project,

■ Participants in the project,

■ Personnel conducting or managing the project, and

■ A timeline of events.

It might be helpful to list the activities with a timeline or on a chart so that you can describe your plan in chronological order. Computer software can make chart-making a breeze.

Budget

This section includes a financial description of your project with explanatory notes. One page will be the budget sheet, and the other will be the budget narrative. Most RFPs include a specific form sheet upon which to record your budget plans. In addition to the budget sheet, there is usually a budget narrative in which you must accurately state what funds you will need and how you are planning to spend them.

What will the financial requirements for your project be? The grantor will want to see realistic figures and a realistic timeline for making expenditures. The grantor will also want to know how you are going to keep track of funds and record progress.

Phases

If your project will occur in phases, be sure to note the estimated costs associated with each phase. Make sure the grantor understands why you need the outside funding. Try to anticipate questions like "Why can't you use your school district funds for these items?"

In-Kind

Some RFPs require a list of in-kind budget items your institution will provide. This request refers to the services or supplies that will be provided by you, your media center, your school, or your district. An example of an in-kind service would be donating your time and talent to conducting an evening workshop for parents to help them read aloud to their children. If you would not be paid for the workshop, your services would be an in-kind contribution to the project. Parents volunteering their time would be another example. In-kind contributions can be considered a method of cost-sharing.

Categories

Organize your budget expenses into major categories:

- Materials or supplies,
- Equipment,
- Salaries,
- Employee benefits and FICA payments,
- Travel,
- Consultants, professional services and contracts,
- Personnel,
- Communications, and
- Publicity and publications.

Estimate Accurately

Don't underestimate your budget needs. If you do, the grantor may think you haven't done your homework. Be realistic; plan for the unexpected. Do careful research. Make phone calls, get online, order price lists. Once you have these figures, you can better estimate your total budget needs. Extra effort and attention will help you avoid underestimating your needs. The granting organization may question your competence in other areas if you cannot accurately predict the financial needs of your project. Then later, if you do get your grant, you may be in trouble when you try to implement the program with inadequate funding. How will you complete your project? Now is the time for you to carefully think through the costs of your project, bearing in mind that it may take as long as a year before you begin to receive funding, and costs may have increased by then. And remember that there are unanticipated costs even in the best-laid plans.

Make It Look Good

Use a spreadsheet format with an appropriate title. Round off your figures to the nearest $10, $50 or $100. Set your spreadsheet program to align the figures and provide subtotals within each section. Consider using a money management software program to help you develop your budget.

Salaries

Be cautious about budgeting salaries of new employees in your proposal. Once the grant has ended, who will fund those positions? Most school district leaders are leery of seeking grants that commit the school district to funding new staff positions in the future. If you need personnel help, can you pay stipends to employees already on the payroll? Can you contract with a consultant for services and then not be obligated for future expenses once the services have been performed?

Many grant proposal writers suggest that you avoid requesting funds for hiring staff when you can. If you do request additional staff, how will you sustain funding for that position in the long range? Usually, your school district will not be interested in adding positions.

Other Costs

Don't forget to include postage, office supplies, printing, and the like. Make sure your budget contains no unexplained amounts. Keep records of how you arrived at your budget figures. You will need them if budget modifications are required or if your budget is questioned.

Make Changes Carefully

Be careful as you progress in writing your proposal. When you make changes in your proposal, remember to make corresponding changes in your budget. It is easy to change parts of the proposal and forget to change the budget section. Few things can turn a grantor off faster than a budget that does not match the proposal.

Multiple Funding Sources

If you plan to have multiple funding sources, note that in your budget. Be careful to describe funds from other entities that you have already secured for your project. Include a time line in your budget. When will your other funds arrive and for how long a time period will they be available?

Be Honest

Be financially honest; do your budget homework carefully. Include legitimate in-kind services and genuine funding from other sources. Be fair. Don't short-change yourself, but don't even think of padding the budget.

Use the Generic

In normal circumstances, you will write your budget using generic terms, not brand names. Although you may want to specify the platform of your computer, PC or MAC, you will probably want to write your budget using generic terms, such as "computer workstation."

Cautions

Requesting funds to pay stipends for teachers or consultants is reasonable. Don't forget to include funds for benefits such as health care and Social Security. Detail those fringe benefits separately from salaries.

Without specific permission from the superintendent and school board, do not obligate your school or school district to spend money in order to accept a grant. Beware of the phrase "matching funds." Do not apply for anything requiring matching funds from your school system without the permission of the powers that be.

Mention major budget expenditures within the body of your proposal so that the budget section makes good sense to the reader. See Appendix M for a sample budget.

Be aware that you may need to adjust your budget later. It is not uncommon for a proposal to be considered for funding provided that the budget is modified according to the donor's specifications. Be open to new ideas and ways of executing your project, if the need arises.

Personnel

The benefactors want to know who the key players in your grant are. In the personnel section, you will provide a brief description of your staff—number of full-time paid staff members, part-time staff members, and volunteers. Include only information relevant to this project.

Credentials

You will ordinarily write a paragraph describing the credentials and special skills of each of the participants in the grant. You may need to include resumes or curricula vitae of all the participants. Summarize your school's or your district's expertise and show how it supports your proposal.

If, for instance, your principal, the head librarian at the local community college, and you are writing this grant together, those are the people you will highlight in the personnel section, listing all their pertinent degrees, certifications, and awards.

One of your objectives in this section is to establish your credentials and demonstrate why you are capable of accomplishing this project. Make sure the grantor understands that you are a member of a viable organization (your school), that you have a good solid idea, and that you are a capable project manager. Tell why you are uniquely qualified to solve the problem your project is designed to solve. The benefactor wants to know your track record. If you have received other grants, list them.

Job Descriptions

Include job descriptions if the RFP or application contains those requirements.

Resumes

If you are applying for and implementing the grant yourself, include your resume. See the sample resume in Appendix G. There are many other excellent resume samples and helpful sites on the Internet; CareerBuilder.com is one.

You may want to save more than one version of your resume in your database. Some of your credentials will be more relevant to one project than to another. Tailor a version of your resume for the intended project.

Don't forget to include examples of your leadership and management skills—serving as PTA president or church stewardship campaign chairman, for instance, but don't list every committee you ever served on or every continuing education class you ever took. Strive for balance.

Keep your resume to one page. Assume your reader is a busy person. If your project is larger, you will probably need to include the resumes of other grant project participants in the appendix section.

Biographical Sketches

Some applications ask for biographical sketches instead of resumes. A biographical sketch includes the same information as a resume but is written in third-person narrative form. Think about an author profile on a book jacket. That image will help you get started writing about yourself in third person. Keep it short (one page or less), focus on your career, and include only the most significant and pertinent information.

Evaluation

You need a method of evaluating the results of your project. This section of your proposal is critical to your success. Experts say that more points are lost here than in almost any other section, so proceed with caution. Conversely, a good evaluation plan will help you win your grant. Clear, understandable evaluation findings will help build support for your program from your administration, your district, and your community. They will increase the sustainability of your project.

Formative or Summative

There are two ways to evaluate a project's effectiveness: Either analyze the process that you have put into place or measure some type of product. A process evaluation is a *formative evaluation*. A product evaluation is a *summative evaluation*.

The evaluation process you choose can be critical to your success. Tie it to your objectives. Keep the process simple and manageable while making it meaningful. Ask yourself:

■ Will the project impact student test scores?

■ What tests or measurements do your students already take that could be used to measure the effect of the grant project?

■ What products or results will the proposed project yield?

■ How could they be used to evaluate the project's impact?

■ Can you display the data on charts or graphs as evaluation data?

Using test data that your school already gets is a low-cost, effective project evaluation tool. You could also use performance-based assessment or portfolios. What process will you be implementing with the grant project that could be evaluated? Sorry, anecdotal information is no longer considered meaningful in program evaluations.

Would your circulation statistics serve as an evaluation measurement? Will your library circulation figures increase as a result of the grant project? Will the reading teacher need to give an informal reading inventory to the students before and after your project? Is she willing to do that and does your principal support that assessment? Do you need special permission from parents to test? Do you need to budget for the cost of the tests and their administration?

Other ways of collecting data are interviews, observations by staff or experts, and examination of records.

Evaluating Technology

If your proposal is for some type of educational technology, remember that technology is a means to an end—learning. Technology is not an end unto itself. If you are asking for technology for students, be prepared to show what increase in student achievement can be expected and how you will measure it. If you are requesting high-tech equipment, make sure your plan is student-centered. What data will you use to demonstrate that your students have progressed academically as a result of your project? Will they be able to make better grades, score higher on tests or other assessments, complete more challenging coursework, demonstrate mastery of skills? How can that be measured? Does the technology make learning easier? If so, how can you measure it? What overall impact will the project have on student achievement and how can that be measured?

Test Resources

If you want to use test data and need more information about existing evaluation instruments, take a look at Buros' *The Seventh Mental Measurements Yearbook*, published by the University of Nebraska Press. This two-volume set lists tests in many fields and describes each test. The ISBN# is 0803211600, and the Buros Web site is <http://www.unl.edu/buros>. Another resource for testing instruments is the two-volume *ETS Collection Catalog*, published by the Educational Testing Service, Orynx Press, ISBN#s 0897747437 and 089774893X, Web site <www.ets.org>.

Another helpful resource is *An Educator's Guide to Evaluating the Use of Technology in Schools and Classrooms*. Sherri Quinones and Rita Kirshstein wrote this U.S. Department of Education Office of Educational Research and Improvement publication, which includes many useful evaluation tools. Ask for report ORAD-1999-12.

Evaluation Methods

Your sponsor wants to know that the grant dollars will be well spent. You will typically need to provide evidence of the impact of the grant on your population at the end of the grant period. Try to keep the measurement of impact as simple as possible. Following are some evaluation methods to consider:

■ Test scores,

■ Circulation,

■ Number of visits to the library,

■ Traffic on your Web site,

■ Staff development,

■ Parent, staff, or student survey,

■ Feelings of competency, and

■ Improved self-confidence.

Interim Reports

You may be asked to provide both interim and final reports describing your project. These reports may fulfill a type of evaluation requirement. A typical report would include budget expenditures, attendance or enrollment records of project participants, summaries of accomplishments, and other data. I strongly recommend that you commit to submitting an interim report.

Evaluation Consultation

If you do not feel confident writing the evaluation section of your proposal, consider contacting a colleague in higher education to ask for assistance or guidance. One of the keys to designing an evaluation section is to make sure you have meaningful and measurable objectives. That will make writing your evaluation component much easier.

Review Other Evaluation Components

Another source of help is the evaluation sections of successful grant proposals. The best ones are specific and meaningful, not vague and unfocused. If there will be a cost associated with your evaluation component, include it in your budget. Keep it simple. The grantor wants to know if the project worked.

- Identify what will be evaluated,
- Decide the method of evaluation to use,
- Employ the method, and
- Analyze and summarize the data.

Timeline

Many RFPs ask for a detailed timeline; usually, the larger the grant, the longer the project takes to complete. While a $500 grant may have a very simple time line, a $200,000 grant will require a more elaborate one. The $500 grant project may take a semester, while the $200,000 one may span two or three school years.

Dissemination

Most RFPs today ask the grantee to delineate a plan by which the project and its results can be shared with a wider audience, thus multiplying its value. Some dissemination strategies are

- Project newsletter,
- Workshops designed to share the project,
- Site visits,

- Interim and final reports on the progress of the project,
- Presentations at local, state, regional, national, and international conferences,
- Journal articles,
- Informative brochures,
- Demonstrations of methods and materials, and
- Press conferences.

The dissemination section of your proposal should identify

- A time line for dissemination activities,
- Personnel responsible for dissemination,
- Budget for dissemination activities,
- Target audience for the dissemination information,
- Methods for distributing printed materials, and
- Methods for evaluating the dissemination activities.

Sustainability

Some grant applications require you to describe the sustainability of your proposed project. Even if there is no specific section for this, it's best to cover this topic somewhere in your proposal. The benefactor wants to know that, once the seed money is gone and you've cashed the final grant check, your organization can sustain the project. Once the grant is completed, will you need additional funding or can your regular budget support the project?

Letters of Support

Many applications request that you submit letters of support. If you are collaborating with another local entity, the funding organization wants evidence of support from upper management of both organizations. They want to know if your principal, your superintendent, and parent organization supports your effort. Letters of support may be required from

- The superintendent of schools,
- The college president,
- The dean,
- The chief operating officer,
- The chief financial officer,
- The head librarian,
- The director of curriculum and instruction,

- The chairperson of the school site council,

- The president of the PTA,

- The president of the teachers' association,

- Your city's mayor,

- Someone from the state department of education who is familiar with your accomplishments as they relate to this project.

Not all letters of support are created equal. You be the judge, but consider not including letters that are so generic and nonspecific that they lend no weight to your cause. Do include letters that are well written, compelling, and likely to increase your chances of success.

Certification and Signatures

Many grant applications require a form certifying your nonprofit or tax-exempt status. Your school system's business office can help you with IRS Form 501(c)3 and other documentation to meet this requirement.

Many applications require the signature of the head of your organization—usually the superintendent of schools. Plan ahead to get the necessary signatures.

Attachments, Supporting Documentation, and Appendixes

Some RFPs will specify types of attachments you may include with your proposal. A brochure about your library, one describing your school, and a third describing your district might be appropriate. If you don't already have these brochures, don't feel you need to produce them for the project.

If there is a recent news article about your school and it is relevant to your project, include it. Other attachments might be

- Organizational charts,

- Fiscal reports or budgets,

- Agency publications,

- Award descriptions,

- Diagrams or schematics of proposed equipment requests, and

- Your school's report card, if your state issues them.

Attach only carefully selected items that directly support your proposal, and attach nothing unless the RFP specifically requests it. Don't make more work for your proposal reader. Highlight pertinent sections of journal or newspaper articles to make them easier to read. Most grant application readers don't have time to watch that video you want to send; in fact, an unsolicited video can be irritating. If in doubt about a possible attachment, consult the guidelines in the RFP. Check to make sure that you have included everything the granting organization requests and send it in the form requested.

Tip: Set Interim Due Dates

Even if you are working on your own without a grant-writing team, you still need interim due dates. Keep yourself motivated by setting short-term goals. Reward yourself with a cold soda or a hot coffee or some token pleasure when you meet your short-term goals. You must keep yourself motivated in order to conquer this beast.

Sample Grant Proposals

There are many examples on the Internet of successful grant proposals. Log on to one of the Web sites, such as Scholastic.com teachers' site, and read some of the proposals. You can find the Scholastic examples at <http://teacher.scholastic.com/professional/grants/sampropo.htm>. Reading proposals that have been funded is an excellent way to learn your way around the sections of a grant proposal.

Chapter 6

Speak Clearly

Your manuscript is both good and original, but the part that is good is not original and the part that is original is not good.

—**Samuel Johnson**

If you mean *school principal*, say *school principal*, don't say *head learner*. Define your terms. You have a clear understanding of what brain-based education, authentic assessment, and curriculum-based measurement mean, but don't assume the grant proposal reader does. Educational grant application reading teams almost always include members from business and government, not just educators. A good rule of thumb is to write your proposal so that your mother can understand it, even if she is not a schoolteacher.

In good writing there is no substitute for clarity—not big words, not sentence length, not type style or size. The easier your proposal is to read, the more likely it will be thoroughly read. The harder you make it for the reader to understand your project, the less likely it is that your plan will be read, understood, and funded.

Hook Your Reader from the Beginning

One of your objectives should be to clearly establish who you are and what your goals are. Tell the reader why you have credibility in the project area you are proposing, then lead directly into the statement of need. Write simply and to the point. Shine the spotlight on your ideas.

There is no time like the beginning to capture the reader's interest. Start with a powerful image for the need you propose to fill, or a persuasive testimonial or quote from a student. Provide concrete examples. Your objective is to show the reader why your project or idea is unique.

Another way to capture the reader's attention is to begin with a question. "How can one school library make a difference in the digital divide? At Sunny Skies School library, we think we have an answer . . ."

Define Terms

If you are going to use an educational term, define it initially in as few words as possible and illustrate with an example. For instance, "*Service learning* is a teaching method that combines service to a community with a standard K–12 academic curriculum. As part of their schoolwork, students perform community projects in order to build both academic skills and civic responsibility."

If you need to use technical terms, don't assume your reader understands them. Translate them into ordinary language. Team members who review grant proposals come from a variety of fields. While another school librarian might know just what you mean, a coordinator of vocational technical programs may not.

Spell out Acronyms the First Time

If you want to refer in your proposal to your library media center as the LMC, start by spelling the words in full, followed by the acronym in parentheses. Subsequently throughout the document, you may refer to it as the LMC. Beware of using too many acronyms. The lay reader has a hard time with alphabet soup. While you may know that ELL refers to students who are new English Language Learners, assume that your grant reader has never heard the term.

Avoid Jargon

It is easy for educators to get into the habit of using educational jargon. When they begin to speak in the jargon of their profession, noneducators can be clueless. While to an educator, *special education* may mean a specific educational program mandated by law for students who have an individualized educational program (IEP), those words may mean nothing specific to a lay grant application reader. To avoid having to define too many terms, stay away from jargon. If you mean *school*, use the word *school*, not *attendance center*.

Make It Simply the Best

The person assigned to read and score your grant proposal probably has a stack of several grant proposals to read and score. Do the reader a favor by keeping yours easy to read. Picture in your mind motivational, high-interest/low-vocabulary books. Hold that mental picture when writing your grant. Make your proposal a high-interest, easy-to-read document.

The reader isn't interested in how intelligent the grant writer is or what big words she knows. He wants to know what the money is needed for, what is going to be done for the kids with that money, and what is the plan to measure the results.

Make sure there is plenty of meat on the bones of your proposal; leave the fat for another project. Picture yourself writing a lean and enduring proposal using short, meaningful sentences. More pages and multisyllabic words do not equate with a better chance at funding. Keep your proposal simple and crystal clear. Your reader will value your brevity and precision.

Avoid Redundancy, Cliches, and Fluff

As you make your case, say it once and say it well. Saying the same thing six different ways does not endear yourself to your reader. Be aware that the proposal may ask you for the information in more than one section. Furnish the information in each section where it is requested, modifying but not embellishing the language. Proofread to eliminate repetition.

Again, I want to remind you not to make the same point over and over again until your reader is sick of hearing about the point that you are making. Try not to be redundant and say things over and over again. The reader gets really tired of reading when you make the same point over and over again. Remember, don't be redundant or say the same things over and over again. Get my point?

Find Synonyms

Reread what you have written. Are you using the same tired words over and over? Can you find suitable synonyms for them? Does your software have a thesaurus? Don't beat a dead horse, feel the benefactor's pain, or smell the roses. Avoid using words like **nice**, **great**, **wonderful**, and **absolutely**; they're overused and tired. As you edit your first draft you will probably find that you have included a few clichés and some tired words. What do you really mean? Take the trouble to find the precise adjective or an original metaphor. It's hard to be trite when you're being scrupulously specific.

Provide Examples

They make your grant proposal come alive. When you paint a vivid picture with your words, you put some fizz in your proposal. If you want computers with Internet access for your students, describe the students surfing the NASA site to learn about science experiments in space. Then show how the students, as a result of this project, will benefit the community. Hollywood claims that nothing sells a story like a kid or a dog. You have the kids. Use them to sell your idea. Grantors want to know that their money will make a difference in the lives of children.

Avoid sounding arrogant or overconfident. Don't talk down to the reader or try to obfuscate something that you would prefer the reader not discern. Avoid using controversial language.

Consider Your Reader

Just as some people talk too much, some people use too many words when writing. Say what needs to be said, but leave out the fluff and the filler. When a proposal has been stuffed with jargon and padded with verbiage, the alert reader wonders, "Where's the beef?" Substance yes, window dressing no.

Words are telling and readers are bright.

Use a Consistent Style and Format

Find a Voice

Find your writer's voice and use it consistently throughout the grant proposal. Avoid switching from first person to second person to third person.

If you are fortunate enough to have a team writing the proposal, one person must take on the job of putting the several contributions into one voice. The final document should read as though it were written from start to finish by one person. Achieving this uniform voice is difficult, but without it you jeopardize your proposal's credibility.

Speak Clearly

Use precise language. Take the newspaper *USA Today* as a model. Their writers write so that the average citizen can read and comprehend. Erudition and extensive matriculation are impressive in graduate school. Plain speaking goes a long way with an overburdened grant reader. Make clarity and precision your goals.

Use the active voice. Instead of "The run was scored by Big Rex," write, "Big Rex scored the run!"

Transition Words Phrases for Coherence

Use all the tips your former English teachers taught you in order to help your reader follow your train of thought. Begin each new section with a strong introductory sentence and wording that tells the reader where it fits in your overall plan; for instance, "Our third indicator that something needed to be done came in the spring of 2002. . . ." As you move from paragraph to paragraph and section to section, provide transition words and phrases: *first, next, and then, finally.*

Think of alternate ways to say something that must be repeated. Linking expressions are numerous: *in conclusion, to conclude, to sum up, finally, in short, hence, therefore, furthermore, another, moreover, at last.*

Use connecting words to show the relationship among ideas, details, and sections of your proposal. Some common transitional words and phrases are

after	*after that*	*also*
another	*as a result*	*at the same time*
besides	*consequently*	*finally*
for example	*for instance*	*however*
in addition	*instead*	*later*
likewise	*otherwise*	*similarly*

Use the Language of the Grantor

This is one of my favorite grant-writing tips. As you carefully read the grant application, remember that you highlighted the key words or phrases your potential benefactor used. Now is the time to incorporate those words within your own proposal. When members of the grant review committee spot those words, they'll sense they have a winner. Bing, bing, bing, fifty points!

Describe or State Precisely

How could you say, "A lot of students will benefit greatly" in a more precise manner? Could you say, "All 537 students at Happy Days School will be scheduled to use the computer lab a minimum of one hour per week to practice their writing skills?"

It is critical to be specific in your budget section. The donor cares deeply how grant funds will be spent. For example, *"Travel - $500"* does not paint an accurate picture. *"Purchase a round trip airline ticket at $250 each for two authors to travel from Jonesville to Springfield in April"* is much clearer. Specificity in budget writing is supremely important.

Be Compelling and Fresh

The grantor and the grant application reader are human beings. While your proposal must present the facts, you must also persuade the reader to choose your project for funding. Humanize your proposal, but don't go overboard. Put some emotion in the draft without making it a sob story. Use dramatic details that illuminate the situation you are describing. Avoid exaggeration and overstatement. Don't promise more than your project can deliver.

Find a way to allow your personality, your heart, and your energy to shine through your words without overpowering your good ideas. After a reviewer reads so many proposals, the words on the page can begin to look like "blah, blah, blah." If your commitment to your students and community are genuine, find a way to let that energy and commitment shine through.

Readers love a surprise or a puzzle when it is presented well. It provides a mental oasis in a desert of dry proposals. After reading a number of grant applications, the reader becomes numb to the standard pattern of the document. The art of grant writing makes a difference when the writer adds something that makes a proposal resonate with the reader.

Appearance Does Matter

The layout of your proposal can also make a powerful statement about your organizational skills and clarity of thought.

Graphics

Many readers prefer graphic representations of complex ideas. Use a chart, graph, or timeline to demonstrate your concept whenever possible. You can save words and clarify complex descriptions by using a well-done graphic.

Paint a clear picture with the statistics; don't put the reader to sleep. Use bullets and charts, instead of wordy sentences, to show your needs.

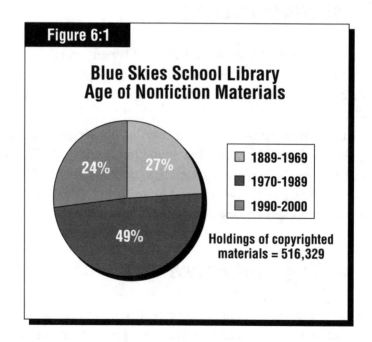

Figure 6:1

**Blue Skies School Library
Age of Nonfiction Materials**

24% 27% 49%

- ☐ 1889-1969
- ■ 1970-1989
- ☐ 1990-2000

**Holdings of copyrighted
materials = 516,329**

A time-and-task chart can be helpful to demonstrate project activities and time line. Consider searching for a graphic organizer that will help your reader better understand your ideas.

White Space

Plan to provide your overworked proposal reader with plenty of white space. Use headings and subheading and make them **bold**. Avoid <u>underlining</u>, using ALL CAPITAL LETTERS or *italics*. Those devices all make a document more difficult to read.

White space makes it easier for the reader to skim for important details. Leaving plenty of white space in your document makes your proposal more reader-friendly and sends mental signals that one topic or section is ending and another is beginning. White space provides transition space for the reader's brain to shift from one unit of information to another. Beware; the dense underbrush of too many words can bury your good ideas.

Lists and Headings

One way you can provide white space and get your reader to focus on the main point is to use lists. Lists make it easier for the reader to skim the sections of your proposal. Use a numbered list when items need to be understood in a specific order. Use bullets if sequence is not significant. Lists can save you words, and that is critical if there is a word limit for your proposal.

Headings help the reader keep a sense of order. They act as graphic organizers and help the reader go quickly back to previous information when a question arises. Headings are a courtesy to the reader; they open the door to the next section. They help maintain adequate white space and show that you respect the reader's valuable time.

After the reviewer has read a proposal once, she usually needs to read it again. Having subject headings and subheadings in place allows her to skim the document for necessary information—almost like a table of contents to the hurried reader.

Headings and subheadings should always match the headings in the RFP, where applicable. If you have the grantor's scoring rubric as part of the application, you can see where the reviewer will be awarding points. Make sure your subject headings correspond to that rubric and stand out. In other words, help the reviewer decide in your favor.

Spacing and Margins

Double spacing is standard for grant proposals unless the guidelines request otherwise. Double spacing provides the reader with more white space for clarity and readability. Single-spaced lines are difficult to read; they are more likely to produce headaches and eyestrain.

Unless otherwise specified, leave the right margins ragged. Do not "right align" the text in the body of your proposal. Right-alignment produces irregular spacing within the line, and that is distracting to the reader. Ragged right margins make reading easier.

Font, Type Size, and Pagination

Type size should be large enough to read comfortably; 12-point is standard. (There are 12 points in one pica and 6 picas in one inch.) Tiny print may allow you to get more words into your proposal, but those words won't do you much good if the reader can't read them. Check the grant application specifications carefully for required type size. If none is given, use no smaller than 10 points. Do your best to make the document comfortable for the eye of the reader.

The type style, or font, may be stipulated in the proposal guidelines. If it is not, use a common, standard, easy-to-read font. Type style is not a place to be highly original. Save the swirly o's and squiggle letters for your scrapbook, not a formal grant proposal.

The pages of your proposal should be numbered. Page numbers are most easily read when they are at bottom center or at top right of the page. Do not number the title page or the first page of the document. Use an alternative pagination system, such as lower-case Roman numerals for the appendix and table of contents.

Avoid Fancy

Don't be tempted to put bells and whistles in your proposal. Although you want your proposal to stand out from the rest, you want it to stand on the merit of its content, not its shiny red cover and microchip that plays "Jingle Bells" when the cover is open. Save fancy notebooks, folders, and bindings for your family albums.

Big notebooks or three-ring binders can be a nuisance to the receiver. They are more expensive to mail and difficult for the recipient to store. The grant proposal should follow the grantor's guidelines and be stapled or paper-clipped just as requested.

Plan Ahead

Writing a winning proposal takes time. Give yourself the luxury of plenty of time to write, edit, and rewrite your proposal. If you know that a grant competition's deadline is one year away, you'd be wise to begin preliminary work to put your proposal together. If you hear about a competition that is due two weeks from today, applying for it is probably not a viable option for this round. Writing a grant takes time. Allow yourself about three months to write a first draft, edit, and revise.

Tip: Write and Rewrite

In order to produce a quality grant proposal, it will be necessary to write and rewrite the proposal several times. Writing is a process, and rewriting is a vital facet of that process. It is important to get the first draft done before the rewrite begins. Metaphorically speaking, let it get cool before you slice and dice it.

The following list summarizes this chapter:

- Hook the reader at the start.
- Define terms; spell out acronyms at first mention.
- Avoid jargon, redundancy, clichés, filler, and fluff.
- Use short sentences.
- Be brief, precise, and say it once.
- Use transitions to keep your reader with you.
- Choose meaningful words and give clear examples.
- Use relevant statistics.
- Speak the language of your prospective benefactor.
- Keep visual concerns in mind.
- List and highlight; use consistent formatting.
- Take a fresh approach.
- Reread and revise.
- Use your language skills to make your grant stand out from others.

Chapter 7

Edit Until It Hurts

It requires more than mere genius to be an author.

—**Jean de la Bruyere,** *Les Caracteres de Theophraste* **(1688)**

Get your ideas written down, make sure you have met the RFP's guidelines, and then put your first draft aside for a day or two. This way, you'll reread it with fresh eyes as you start to revise. For you will need to read and revise it several times before you are ready to take it to the editor.

Read, Reread, Write, and Rewrite

Once a proposal is written, it is necessary to read it over and over. If you are doing your job properly, you will have read and reread it so many times that you've begun to memorize it. If you can put it aside for a few days between readings, you'll find each time that you've left out something pertinent.

You'll also rewrite several times. Don't be discouraged. Remember, writing is a process, and rewriting is an important facet of it. You will improve your document each time you revise it.

Title It

A catchy title is a major asset to your proposal. *Hola Dr. Seuss* was the title of a winning application from a media specialist who wanted Spanish language books for her elementary library. *Spanish Language Books for the Highlands Media Center* just doesn't carry the cachet of *Hola Dr. Seuss*. The proposal review team continually referred to *Hola Dr. Seuss* as they considered the projects. The title was catchy and easy to remember. It hooked the readers. They smiled as they repeated it, *"Hola Dr. Seuss,"* again and again during the review process.

Headings and Lists

Look for ways to put in meaningful headings and subheadings. They help the reader see at a glance the organization of your paper and spot the main points.

Read again to see if you can eliminate long sentences by making lists. For example, "We will gather input from

- Students,
- Staff,
- Parents,
- Administration, and
- Community."

Tip: Add Pagination

Add pagination when you are editing. Bottom center of each page or upper right hand corner are the prime spots for page numbers.

Revise It for Mechanics and Content

Let a few days go by and read the manuscript again to see if you can reduce it, rearrange it, and rewrite it to improve its clarity. Ask an educator to proofread and edit your proposal. Educators are great at finding errors and can also help with content suggestions.

Flesh It Out

As you reread it, you will see where more flesh is needed on the bones of your proposal and where there are holes in your argument. Where would an example help make your points? Add substance until the proposal is clear and convincing even to someone completely outside your field.

Give It Punch

Find a way to make your grant proposal stand out from the rest. You can't print your grant on colored paper, but you can use colorful language. You can tell a powerful story and hook your reader. Remember how a good murder mystery captures your attention from the first page by delivering a juicy murder right off? Blast off with a personal story, a colorful example, or a question.

Make the necessary statistics interesting. Clarify your argument with statistics, but don't put the reader to sleep. A testimonial from a fellow teacher, a quote from a student, or a note of thanks from a parent could make your proposal come to life.

Dr. Beverly Nichols wrote a proposal for a consortium of four elementary schools for a half-million-dollar, three-year, Disney Learning Partnership grant whose objective was to find innovative approaches to teaching and learning. Her title was $A^2\ I^2$: Active Assessment-Integrated Instruction. In the opening paragraphs, she described the problem and proposed response:

Scenario: It is late April—parent conference time at All-America Elementary School. In a sixth-grade classroom, Mark exhibits great pride in his work as he explains to his parents what he has accomplished during the year. His teacher sits quietly by, ready to offer support or further explanation as Mark talks about the various pieces of work he has selected to share. He displays his "country" project, in which he described in considerable detail the country he had chosen to research. He tells his parents about the research he has conducted using multiple library skills; he talks about using time in science class to study the environmental impact brought about by industry in that country; he shows the graphs he has created in mathematics class to compare the various ethnic groups in the country. Mark shows his parents the project description that he and his classmates used to guide their work; the project description included scoring guidelines so that all students knew exactly what was required of them. In addition to the big project, Mark talks to his parents about how his writing has improved during the year and how his problem-solving skills have increased.

Down the hall, in a lower grade, Emily shows her parents selected mathematics papers that she has collected over the year that demonstrate for her parents how her fractions skills have developed. She describes to her parents the different kinds of activities and assessments in which the class was involved on the way to becoming adept at fractions. Her music teacher had included fractions while teaching the class about quarter, eighth, and sixteenth notes. Her art teacher had used fractions in projects that featured proportional enlargements.

In a second-grade room, a beaming eight-year-old plays two audiotapes, one made early in the year and the other just last week. Jose points out to his parents how much better he can read now than at the beginning of the year.

Question: Could scenarios like this one—where students lead conferences that feature student-centered assessment and integrated learning—be happening in any of our schools across the country?

Answer: Yes.

Question: Is this happening with frequency?

Answer: No.

That powerful opening was part of what persuaded the reviewers to select that project for funding.

Be specific

Let the narrative flow. Avoid generalities such as "a lot," "many," "really big," and other nonspecific words and phrases. Too many generalities make your proposal float in a sea of words. Anchor your points with solid information and precise language.

Read your proposal aloud to yourself. Does it flow smoothly? If not, could you improve the transitions from topic to topic, section to section? Does the rhythm of your words make you stumble? Are like ideas expressed in parallel structures? Revise until the narrative flows.

You Can't Overdo Proofreading

Read your proposal again and again, looking at it each time from a different aspect. Look for content. Is your proposal beefy enough, or do you need to add substance and weight?

What about the mechanics? Put on your best English-teacher glasses and look for split infinitives, faulty parallelism, passive voice, subject-verb agreement problems, and spelling errors. How about typos? Did you type "you" when you meant "your"? Have you used these antonyms correctly? How about "there," "their," and "they're," and "to," "too," and "two"?

You selected your words with great care, but once more, reread your draft for word choice. Did you use the same tired words over and over? Try once more to find suitable synonyms for them.

Remember that thesaurus in your software? Use it to check nuances of meaning and to find synonyms for words you've overused. That old grammar or composition textbook may still come in handy. If in doubt on a point of style, consult the *Publication Manual of the American Psychological Association*, the accepted style guide for many grant proposal writers.

How about tone? Ask a friend to read it and tell you if it sounds arrogant, overconfident, or condescending—a definite turn-off to your prospective reader.

Proofread for the logic of your argument. Have you stated the need coherently and provided enough research to support your plan? Is the argument persuasive, or do you need to add an example and cite an authority?

Your finished proposal should be so polished it is ready for publication. How your proposal looks and reads is a critical measurement of your professional skills. Even though proposal writing is probably not part of the project for which you are seeking funding, it is what the grantor has to use to gauge your credibility.

Try an experiment. Let your proposal sit awhile, then come back to read it again. Did your key message come through when you read it? Did you feel the power of the argument? If not, get to work revising it until your message is clear. Ask yourself: If you were the reviewer, would you remember the title of your grant proposal? Would you remember its essence? If you can honestly say yes, then you've met the goal for substance.

Two Essentials: An Editor and a Proofreader

Now it's time to put your proposal before more objective eyes. Don't try to be your own editor. If you've written a good proposal, a professional editor can make it great. Ideally, you'll be part of a writing team that includes an editor. If you don't have that luxury, no matter. You still need an editor.

If possible, get help from both within and outside your organization. Could you volunteer to help a colleague with a project in exchange for his editing yours?

Especially after several rereadings, our brains fill in words that are not really there. Here's where a proofreader comes in. Find a peer who will proofread as well as one who will edit for you—people whom you can trust to care for and nurture your brainchild. Give the proofreader a copy of the RFP so that she can also watch for procedural errors.

Ask questions of your proofreader and editor:

■ What did you not understand?
■ Where do I need to include more information?
■ Where does the proposal sound repetitive?
■ Which parts are too technical?
■ Where is the proposal confusing?

If possible, hire a freelance editor or consultant to proofread or edit your manuscript. The local community college or university may refer you to someone who can proof, edit, and revise it.

Follow Directions to the Letter

Following directions is essential in grant writing. When you serve as a grant reader, you will find it surprising how many grant writers fail to follow the directions. Nothing will end your funding chances faster than failing to do what the directions say. If you are a rebel at heart, get a body part pierced or choose a funky hair color, but follow the grantor's guidelines to the letter. Doing all this hard work only to be eliminated in the first round is demoralizing.

Grant proposals that do not meet the specified criteria do not make it to the finals. If the proposal states that no "bricks-and-mortar" be funded, and you ask for a greenhouse attachment for your media center, you will be rejected.

If the proposal says you may include a specified maximum number of attachments, then follow the directions. If it specifies that the abstract must be limited to one page, then don't make it a page and a half. If the specs say you may not request personnel, don't ask for funding for a library clerk. If you must have three letters of support, then include three, not two or four.

Meet the deadline—no excuses. If you miss the deadline, your proposal will not be considered.

Checklist

You will need a checklist when you are ready to complete your proposal. Include on it all the pertinent information that you have highlighted in the RFP. Go over each section carefully. It might include the following:

❏ Follow application guidelines.

❏ Proofread.

❏ Attach required documents.

❏ Sign all required forms.

❏ Submit requested number of copies.

❏ Meet all deadlines.

If you are allowed to do so, place the title on a header or footer on each page of your proposal. Don't reveal the name of your school or district within the body of the proposal if the guidelines forbid it.

Checking the Budget

Did you complete your budget and then make changes in your proposal plan? If so, did you change the budget to reflect the changes in the plan? Have you checked the math again and again?

Have you met with the powers that be in your district business office? Are they aware of your proposal and supportive of it? Will they have a way of receiving your funds, should you get them, and dispersing them appropriately? Have you dotted all the i's and crossed the t's, just the way the business office likes you to do?

Signatures

Do you have all the required signatures? Do you need an appointment with the superintendent or principal to get his signature? Be sure all copies of your proposal have the requisite signatures. Don't allow all your hard work to go for naught by forgetting to get a required signature and having your project rejected on a technicality. It can be heartbreaking to wait until the last minute and then learn that the superintendent is out of town and not expected back until after your deadline. Plan ahead and get yourself on the calendar of the people who will need to sign your proposal.

If you are doing your homework properly, the signatures will be more than a last-minute formality. You will have kept the key people affected by your project in

---

Tip: Handwriting

Nothing in your application but the signatures should be handwritten. Do not make handwritten corrections. The actual application form should be typed, not handwritten. The appearance of your proposal is extremely important. It should be letter perfect.

the information loop. Each of them will have a clear picture of what your project entails and will have good reason to be supportive. Each will have reviewed the final copy and approved your plan. The signatures will be just the final step.

Appendixes

Gather all the necessary documents for inclusion in the appendixes. If you are working with cooperating organizations, do you have the necessary material from them?

One of the grant proposals we wrote required a copy of our district's five-year plan and technology plan. Both were large and cumbersome documents. The state required several copies of the grant proposal, including the appendixes. One time-consuming job was to get those plans copied and ready for inclusion.

Other appendixes that may be required are:

- A list of other funding sources,
- Financial statements,
- Resumes or biographies of your project team,
- Current budget information,
- Articles about your school or project,
- Equipment specifications,
- Verification of tax-exempt status,
- Photos or clippings, and
- Endorsements or testimonials.

Keep copies of your appendixes as well as of your proposal.

Cover Letter

Do you need a cover letter? Have you written it? On your school or district's letter-head? Is it addressed to the proper recipient?

Copies

Usually, the RFP will ask for duplicate or triplicate copies of your application. You will need a copy of the proposal and appendixes for each member of your grant-writing team, your principal, your superintendent, each cooperating colleague and agency, and the file.

Make more copies than you think you will need. When you are making eight copies of a document, it is easier to make nine than it is to go back and put the whole thing on the copier again. If you are copying newspaper articles for inclusion, cut and paste them to fit nicely on a page. Make sure they are legible. Enlarge or reduce as necessary.

Make sure your copies are clear and legible. If the copier is leaving odd marks on the document, take it to another copier. The appearance of your proposal is very important.

Making the copies of the proposal will be one of the last tasks on your list.

Last-minute changes do occur, so wait to copy the document until all signatures are on it and all changes have been made

Assembly

Fasten each of your document sections with paper clips, binder clips, or staples unless the directions call for some other method of assembly. Do not use a binder unless the RFP requests that you do.

Carefully following the guidelines, you are going to place your cover letter, your proposal, and your appendixes in a manila envelope. Put the packet together in an organized and attractive manner.

Address the envelope to the correct person at the right address. Make your return address legible. You may want to insert an 8 1/2 by 11 piece of cardboard in the envelope to keep the pages stable.

If the guidelines are not clear, call the agency and see if someone there can help you with specific guidelines for assembling and mailing your proposal.

Don't include materials that were not requested. Respect the grantor's requests.

Mailing

You must decide on the best method for getting your proposal to its destination. Ideally, you'll have completed your application in plenty of time to send it by first class mail. If not, non-government delivery companies offer quick service. But consider what it says to the potential benefactor if you use an expensive delivery service. Are you being a good steward of your limited funds? The grantor expects you to be a careful spender.

Editing your proposal and carefully following directions are not very glamorous activities, but they pay off well. Before mailing, check your proposal once more. Have you:

■ Revised and rewritten your first draft?

■ Given your project a catchy title?

■ Put "punch" in your proposal?

■ Written a cover letter?

■ Gotten editing and proofreading help?

■ Followed directions to the letter?

■ Checked with the business office?

■ Gotten signatures?

■ Attached the appendixes?

■ Made copies?

Congratulations

You and your team have completed a major project. The proposal is in the mail. What an accomplishment! It's time to recognize and thank all who have helped.

Turn Rejection into Success

When one door is shut, another opens.

—Miguel de Cervantes, *Don*

I t is wise to have a talk with yourself after you send off your grant application. It may take months before you hear from the grantor. Are you prepared to be patient? And to accept the decision, either way it goes?

Grace is required, whether your project is placed in the winner's circle or outside it. If your project is funded, you'll want to sing it from the rooftops. If the word is not positive, you may wish that the fleas of a thousand camels would infest the grant review team. Neither is a good choice.

Never, ever condemn or berate a potential grantor or a proposal review board. Do not even think about calling the grantor if you're feeling hurt, rejected, or hostile.

Spend some time in front of the mirror, practicing a graceful statement that lets your team know that the project was not funded.

Be Professional

You may feel as if you need a good cry or a little chocolate if you get a "Dear John" letter from the grantor. It is fine to have that moment of downtime, but try to have it in the privacy of your own home with family or a best friend. Put your best professional face on for your administrator, your team members, and your community. You have done a difficult and admirable thing; you have written a grant application. Be proud of your accomplishment.

If you are notified that your grant was not funded, you have permission to feel just a moment or two of rejection. But that is just about all the downtime you get. Do not take the rejection personally. Get back up, dust yourself off, and try again.

Experts say that only about one proposal in ten is funded. It's possible to write a perfect application and still not have it funded.

You put a lot of work in on that grant proposal. That effort isn't for naught. People succeed, not projects. Just the act of working together as a team with your faculty is a unifying force for your school. The energy created by working in collaboration with others gives momentum to your school improvement plan. Identifying needs and solutions, as you have done in writing the grant proposal, can lead to increased support from your school system and community, whether the proposed project is funded or not.

Stay calm. Keep your sense of direction and your determination to get what is best for your students. It takes effort, time, and patience to win grant money. Just completing a grant proposal is an effort worthy of commendation.

Notify Your Team

Remember those wonderful people who worked with you to put this proposal together? They, too, are waiting to hear the news. Your administrator, your staff, your grant-writing team, your editor and proofreader, your volunteers, your collaborating entities and your students—if you told them about the project—are waiting for word from you.

As soon as you can tell them in a dignified and appropriate manner, get to each member of your support team and relay the bad news. If you plan to revise and resubmit in the next round, let them know that too. Tell them how much you appreciated their help and support.

Thank Participants

There is nothing like a handwritten thank-you note for each of your project participants and supporters. Take the time to sit down and write a personal note to each of your team members, thanking her or him for giving time and talent to this project.

Don't forget to thank the grantor, even though your project was not selected. This is an opportunity to build a lasting relationship. Express your appreciation for the person's or organization's philanthropy. Thank the grantor for giving you the opportunity to apply.

Reasons For Rejection

Was your abstract clear? Did you follow directions? Was the budget request reasonable? What can you learn about your application that will enable you to revise and resubmit it? Revision is far less work than starting from scratch. After some time passes, it is easier to get the proposal back out and look at it from a new perspective.

While reasons vary on why your grant might not have been funded, here are some common reasons for rejection:

Misfit. The most frequent reason proposals fail is that they don't match the grantor's specifications or vision. Carefully reading both the application guidelines and the background information about the grantor should help you avoid this error.

Bridesmaid, not a bride. You followed the guidelines but your proposal didn't have the "right stuff" to put you on the winners' pile. Get feedback from someone who has written winning grant proposals. Have a buddy read your proposal and tell you what is great about it and what is not. Then bite the bullet and rewrite your grant proposal.

Budget buster. In the eyes of the grantor, you may have asked for too much money for too small an impact on too few students. Or the grantor may have felt that your budget was too small to make a significant difference for students. Did the grantor set a $150 limit, and you asked for $1,500?

Ask for constructive criticism from the person who notifies you that you were not funded. Sometimes reviewers are reluctant to give you feedback, so be polite and eager to learn; don't challenge their judgment or ask for a point recount.

Me, me, me. Could it be that what you have asked for in your grant proposal benefits the media specialist more than the students? While donors probably like you and want to support you, they want to put their money where the kids are. While a computer in your workroom for you to use exclusively for management might be ideal, the grantor probably won't see it as having a significant impact on students.

Not needy enough. You may not have painted a vivid enough picture of your students' needs. While your project idea may be sound, you have to be crystal clear about the needs of your students. Make the grant-giver feel their pain. Show how funding your proposal will have lasting impact on their lives.

Unwanted proposal. The odds for success are slim when you send a proposal to a grantor who has not asked for it. As in the publishing world, "over-the-transom" submissions have little chance. A letter or call to the granting agency will tell you if you are applying to a likely source.

Insufficient documentation. Does your proposal state that you are working cooperatively with the local community college but lack any documentation of that collaboration?

Frivolous request. Have you asked for a luxury, such as a reading loft for your library, when there are children in your community who lack basic necessities?

Too much for too few. Have you asked for a lot of money to benefit just a few students? Donors like to support projects that make sweeping, vast differences in the lives of as many people as possible. Again, teaming with others will help broaden your base and improve your chances of funding.

Impossible dream. Have you claimed that a storytelling workshop will increase your school's reading scores by five percent? Make sure you can support such a claim with research and statistics.

Weak writing. Face it. Some proposals are not written well, are hard to follow, or lack the power to persuade. The writer may have left out critical information or documentation. The budget may have errors or lack necessary information. Experts say that many grant proposals are rejected because they are poorly written. If you suspect that is why your request was turned down, this is a fixable problem. Seek help.

More reasons for rejection include the following:

- The proposed project would not serve the grantor's target group.
- You have not convinced the grantor of the project designer's qualifications.
- The evaluation plan is weak or nonexistent.
- There is no evidence the plan can be sustained when the project is over.
- The proposal didn't follow the RFP guidelines.
- The grant-seeker's mission and the grant-giver's mission are not in sync.
- The goals are too lofty or too vague.
- The project sounds risky.

Learn From the Experience

You can make the necessary revisions and submit your grant on the next funding round. Go on to land the big one next time, once you have assimilated the information about your current proposal. Remember the little train who thought she could. Don't give up when you are almost at the top of the mountain. Get that proposal off the shelf and look for another potential funding source. Review the progress you have made so far and make a plan to get feedback, modify your proposal, and try again:

- Consider taking a class on grant writing.
- Communicate with your team the status of your proposal.
- Try other donors.
- Get feedback.
- Analyze the reasons your proposal wasn't selected.
- Ask to read a winning proposal.
- Get back up on the horse that bucked you.

Feedback Helps

Accept rejection as a learning experience, gather up your courage, and ask for feedback. Can you find out why your proposal was not selected? Was it too similar to another? Was the budget in line with the grantor's vision?

Don't be discouraged if your proposal is not funded on the first try. Remember, Colonel Sanders sold his recipe on the 1,009th try.

When you ask for feedback, listen carefully. What you hear might make the difference you need to be funded the next time. Think about the feedback for a while. Turn it over in your mind and try to see the criticism from a perspective other than your own. When you've put a lot of hard work into a project, it is natural to defend something so near and dear to your heart. But don't reject criticism; try to learn from it instead.

Take a Class

If your grant was not funded on its first submission, consider taking a grant-writing class or attending a grant-writing seminar before you revise your proposal. This may be a better time to take a course than when you were writing under a deadline. The instructor's words will have more meaning now that you have navigated the waters of grant-writing. Many grant sources offer funding opportunities cyclically. After attending a seminar, you may feel inspired to revise and resubmit your proposal for the next round of competition.

Read a Winner

Ask the grantor's project manager if you may read one of the proposals selected for funding. Read it carefully. Send a thank-you note for the grantor's courtesy. If you cannot read a successful proposal of a fellow applicant, find some examples on the Internet. Print them out and study them. We all need to see and understand a good model before we can hope to produce a winning entry ourselves.

Try Again

Remember all those famous people who suffered rejection and still eventually succeeded? How many times did Lincoln run for office before he was elected? How many times are authors rejected before they sell their first best seller?

Patricia Sellers reported in *Fortune* (May 1, 1995) that Einstein did not speak until age three. Henry Ford went bankrupt with early ventures. An ad agency fired Walt Disney for "singular lack of drawing ability." Babe Ruth struck out 1,330 times—a major league record.

Persevere. Stick to your guns. You can do it. What if Orville and Wilbur had given up after their first failure? We wouldn't be squeezing ourselves into those comfy seats and flying off to fabulous library conferences.

Revise and Recycle

Plan A might be to resubmit the grant proposal to the same entity in the next funding cycle, after editing and revising it. Be sure you get any available feedback from the review of your proposal; try to learn which sections did well and which need help.

Recycling an old grant is much easier than writing a new one. Even recycling an already funded grant to a new grantor is easy. Consider your grant, once written, an asset. You can haul it out, overhaul it, and resubmit it multiple times. Resubmitting a revised version of a nonfunded proposal can bring a good return on your investment of time and effort.

It is possible for a media specialist to get funding from two and three grant sources for the same project. A worthwhile project has lasting, universal appeal. If your grant-funded summer institute was terrific one summer, it could be so again another summer, made possible by a totally different sponsor.

If your lifelong dream is to host a state-wide author's workshop, don't give up at the first rejection. Find out what your proposal scored in each of the sections. Reflect on your weak areas and brainstorm ways to strengthen them. Rework your proposal and resubmit it the next round. Many grants are offered twice a year, most annually, and there is usually no restriction on submitting a revised edition of last year's proposal. Editing, reworking, and rethinking increase your chances of making your dreams come true.

Apply to More Than One Grantor

With a little research, you may find other grant sources to whom you could submit the same proposal with very little modification. If you do submit the same proposal at the same time to more than one fund source, you should communicate that in your project proposal information.

Many large projects are funded by multiple funding sources. Events such as writer's conferences require so much funding and planning that they typically have more than one benefactor. It makes good sense to develop a grant proposal that can be modified or customized for specific money sources.

Chapter 9

Celebrate and Share

Success, remember, is the reward of toil.

—Sophocles, *Electra*

You've just received a grant! Congratulations and best wishes! It is time to celebrate with those who helped make this achievement possible. Personally contact each team member (as well as your boss and superintendent, of course) to share the good news. Let faculty, students, and parents know about it. They will be proud. Call your colleagues at the collaborating institutions.

Next, send a letter of appreciation to your benefactors. Be sure to let them know how thrilled you are and that you are ready to hit the ground running with your project.

Elation, Then Letdown

A letdown feeling may take you by surprise when you hang up the phone from hearing that you have won a grant. You have worked so hard writing your grant and have invested so much time that you're out of steam.

Or you may have written and submitted the grant so long ago that you had almost forgotten it when you were notified of winning. You may find yourself neck deep in alligators of another variety, such as a construction project, state testing, or an all-school flu epidemic. You may ask yourself, "What was I thinking when I asked for this grant?"

Allow yourself to feel a little overwhelmed, overworked, and out of steam. The feeling will pass and your energy will return, but many veteran grant writers confess to feeling a moment's regret when they get what they asked for. After all, winning a grant does mean getting an opportunity to work extra hours and feel more pressure and stress. If you encounter these feelings, remember that soon they will be replaced with a sense of joy and celebration. You will be accomplishing something worthwhile for your students and your school community. It is worth all the hard work to see those test scores rise and your students turn into avid readers.

Get the Word Out

Your stock will be high when the world knows about your Midas touch. The maxim that the rich get richer is true in the world of grants. Once you have the aura of having gotten grant money, people will see you in a new light—a golden light. Perception is reality. When the world knows you have gotten a grant, it will be much easier to get the second one and the one after that. Picture that on your curriculum vita!

Share the Limelight

Don't let yourself be the focus of all the media attention. Spread the accolades among all the participants. Acknowledge your benefactor every chance you get. The grantor justifiably expects to receive a public relations benefit. Most philanthropists, though, have a larger goal: finding a solution to a vexing problem and then disseminating the findings far and wide so as to positively affect the lives of many. Sharing your project with others is a type of civic duty.

Everyone likes positive publicity, including the superintendent of your school district and the mayor of your town. Your winning grant can provide many opportunities to highlight the progress of your school, library, district, students, staff, and families.

Keep a Scrapbook

Once you have won a grant, use a standard three-ring binder and a package of plastic sheet protectors to make a permanent record of such things as

- The grant proposal,
- The notification letter telling you the good news about funding,
- Each of the press releases about your grant,
- Pictures of the participants and events,
- Newspaper and journal clippings, and
- Journal articles about your project.

Continue to put clippings, photos, and other memorabilia in your scrapbook throughout the life of the project. This will be a historic record of the project and provide a treasure trove of information when others have questions about your project. It will also help you as you plan and write more grant proposals.

Share Within Your School

Start your dissemination program right at home. Your project can be shared with your staff on staff development days, school improvement meeting days, in mentoring sessions with student teachers and new teachers, and informally in the teacher's lunchroom.

Posters. Make a poster (or let your creative students do it) for your media center showing what your grant is doing for your library. Did you get money to buy books and backpacks for your preschoolers? Take photos of the children at school and at home reading with parents and showcase them in a colorful poster.

Bookmarks. Make bookmarks about your project to place on your circulation desk.

Share in the Local Community

Contact the local news media through:

Press releases. If your school system has a communications expert or a public relations specialist, give her a call to share the news about your grant. She will probably want to write a press release about your grant. She is likely to have distribution lists and media contacts that will gain maximum exposure for you, your benefactor, and your project. If you don't have a public relations person, get your principal's permission to write a press release yourself and send it to local newspapers and radio and TV stations. A timely fax of a press release each time your project enters a new phase is a sure way to keep your venture in the news.

News conferences. A significant grant may call for a news conference. Your school district administrators will determine if that is appropriate. Let your grant-writing teammates answer some of the questions.

Newsletters. Write a story for your school newsletter as soon as you've gotten the good news. Your colleagues, your students, and their parents will want to know the good news. Give them a succinct account of what you have gotten, from whom, and for what purpose. This is another opportunity to give credit and express appreciation to the grantor.

PTA Meetings. Make sure your PTA is "in the loop" and ask to be placed on the agenda of their next meeting for a short presentation describing your grant project. Be sure and thank the PTA for their support of your media center as you share the good news.

Share Among Your Peers

Let your associations and professional affiliations know about your good news.

Associations. The teacher's association, and your local, state, and national library association and fraternities may want to highlight your good fortune.

Journals. *Library Journal* wants photos of your library hosting special events or kicking off special occasions. Send your photos and news releases to *Library Journal* News, 245 W. 17th St., New York, NY 10011. Other journals dedicated to school libraries might also be interested in your program.

Articles. Once you have written and won a grant and are preparing to implement it, you will have an article in your head, just waiting to be written. If you plan from the very beginning of the process to write an article, you can do several things at the outset to get ready to publish:

- Keep notes.
- Take pictures.
- Save clippings.
- Keep a journal.

Writing an article about the project at its conclusion is a powerful way to disseminate information. Keep good records from the outset; they'll help you write a better article later.

Share in Your Region and Beyond

Project Fact Sheet. Develop a one-page fact sheet about your project. Have it available to give when you have inquiries about your project.

Brochures. Expand your fact sheet to a brochure. Office supply stores have special brochure paper that can make your publication look professional. For a sample brochure, See Appendix K, *"Integration–Assessment, a Partnership with Shawnee Mission Schools and Disney Corporation."*

Make a header or footer in your word-processing software crediting the granting organization, and insert it each time you send out a publication.

Once the Project Is Underway

The positive publicity about your grant must continue throughout the life of the grant. The initial press conference and press release may be great, but the work of communicating about your project must continue.

There are two things you have to share: the method you used to write your winning grant and the impact the grant project has had on your school. People interested in school improvement will be interested in hearing about these accomplishments. In a rising tide, all boats rise. What goes around comes around. When you help your colleagues and neighbors help students, good things will come back to you.

Also, your benefactor has a vested interest in your letting others know about the impact of your grant. One of your civic responsibilities when you receive a grant is to make sure that you provide help and information to people who want to know how to replicate your project. That effort is owed to the grantor.

How can you get the word out about the plan you developed and help others reproduce the effects in other locations? There are several ways.

Volunteer. Volunteer to help if you know a team that is writing a grant. Be willing to help proofread their grant or to check the budget figures if that is what they need. Share the names of people at the state department of education who helped you. Volunteer to serve on the writing team when your school applies for the Blue Ribbon of Excellence Award.

Teach a Class. "Each one teach one" is the rule. When you feel confident you have mastered the art of grant writing and you have information you would like to share with others, consider teaching a class. Successful grant writing is a complex process. Many educators are anxious to learn more about tapping resources for their classes and schools. Sharing that process with others by teaching a class in your school or school district, your region, or at a local community college or university could fulfill a need in your area. Eventually planning to teach a grant-writing class is another reason to keep careful notes as you write and receive grants.

Present. As your project progresses, consider writing a proposal to make a presentation about it at a conference such as the American Association of School Librarians (AASL). Presenting at a conference is a terrific way to showcase your library's accomplishments and your benefactor's mission.

Plan a PowerPoint presentation on how you put your grant project together. Offer to share it at a local or state library conference or for staff development in your school district or diocesan schools. Once you have written proposals and received a grant or two, you have some ideas about applying and getting them. This is knowledge others would like to have. Consider sharing at the national AASL conference or at your local or state school librarians' conference.

You, your students, and your school were fortunate to have received a grant. Now you must share your good fortune with others in a widening circle:

■ *In your school system.* Others will want to know about your project and how to reproduce it in their buildings. Volunteer to present your multimedia presentation at district in-service sessions, back-to-school orientation sessions for other librarians, or at a school board meeting. Be sure that you temper your offers to share with grace and humility—two qualities that take us a long way on the road to success.

- **In the local community.** Your school site council will want to see your multi-media presentation about your project. So might the downtown development council, the Lion's Club, the Rotary, the Parent Teacher Association, the National Education Association leadership team, and many other groups.

- **In your state.** There are many opportunities in your state for you to volunteer to share your project. The slick multimedia presentation you have developed would make an excellent session at your state school librarian's spring conference. Your former professors at library school might appreciate your sharing the presentation with their current MLS students.

- **In your region.** If you collaborated with the social studies teacher to write your grant and develop your project, volunteer to present together with the social studies teacher at the regional conference for teachers of social studies.

- **Nationally.** Volunteer to share your project at the fall conference of school librarians. You could make a difference in the lives of many students by volunteering to share your project with others across the country. Write and submit articles about your project to a variety of school library journals and to online journal publishers.

- **Internationally.** Did you collaborate with the building reading teacher to write your grant? If so, volunteer to present it at the International Reading Association conference or at an international conference of school librarians.

Take Stock

What an accomplishment you have achieved! Stop and take time to reflect:

- Have you made a plan to publicize your project in a manner that will be beneficial to both the grantor and to your project?

- Have you thanked and honored your benefactor as well as your team members?

- Have you volunteered to help others?

- Have you shared the project with others in a variety of forums and venues?

Chapter 10

Follow Through

As long as you are trying your very best,
there can be no question of failure.
—**Mahatma Gandhi,**
Gandhi the Man **by Eknath Easwaran (Random House, 1978)**

I t is critical that you follow through, once you receive your grant. You may find that you are required to sign and return a special letter or grant contract or agreement. Or the grantor may require that your principal or superintendent of schools sign the letter or contract. Read that agreement carefully and make copies of it for your principal, the school system's business office, and any collaborating institutions with which you may be working.

Make note in your calendar system of important due dates, report dates, and other critical information.

One important reason to carefully follow through on your project is that you may want to ask your benefactor to renew the grant or to fund another sometime in the future. Another reason to do your very best to meet all your commitments is that you are establishing your reputation—and few things are more valuable. Find out right away what the grantor requires of you.

Getting Started

Begin by carefully rereading your original proposal. Make a list of things to be done. Next, contact all the people who will be involved with the project and schedule a meeting to review the scope of the project, the budget, and the time line.

If there is equipment to be ordered, get started. Keep your evaluation activities in mind so that you get the necessary technology ordered and the students involved as quickly as possible.

Keep Records

At some point, a final report will be due. You will need to keep excellent documentation to be ready to write that report. When it is time to disseminate the results of your project, you will need accurate data. Start now to keep impeccably accurate records and statistics so you'll have exactly the data you need. It is easy to record information and statistics as the project events occur. It is a nightmare to try to reconstruct the data later if you forgot to record it at the time of the event. There is no problem if at the end of the project you have more data than you need. The reverse, however, is not true.

Budget

How will you receive the funds from your sponsor? Will they go directly into an account at the district business office? Will you need to establish a special account for these funds?

The moment you receive word that your proposal has been funded, set up a method of bookkeeping to keep track of income and expenditures. As you begin to spend money, save the receipts. In order to keep track of your grant funds and expenditures, make a spreadsheet either on the computer or in a notebook. The choice of accounting system is yours, but don't delay in setting up one.

Seek assistance immediately upon receipt of the grant to make sure you are managing the funding in a legal manner and according to school, district, and state policy and law. It is exciting to receive your first check, but you must be fiscally responsible.

Reporting

Whether your grant proposal was a formal government regulation grant or an informal letter to a corporate sponsor, you will need to produce a report for your grantor. There are benefits to giving the grantor interim reports, as well, whether or not they are required. Interim reports help you:

■ See the progress you are making,

■ Keep you focused and on track,

■ Keep you on schedule, and

■ Help you keep track of loose ends.

An interim report might be as simple as a phone call to your funding organization's program manager. If you have to change an activity in your project, call and let the grantor know.

Final Report

Your project will probably require a final report. The grantor may give you specific guidelines for the final report, or you may be on your own in designing it. Seek help and advice if you have questions.

Find out to whom the report should be addressed and where it should be sent. Determine if there is a specific due date for the report and what documents should be sent with it.

If for any reason you are going to be late with your report or if you have to make budget changes during the project, be sure to alert the grantor. If your evaluation component is delayed for some reason (maybe the test answer sheet-scanning equipment broke down), call the grantor's program manager and discuss it. If you anticipate a delay, give an estimated new date that you'll furnish the data.

Oversight Committee

One option you may wish to consider is to form an oversight committee to help you oversee the implementation of the grant. Depending on the size of your grant and the complexity of the project, an oversight committee of colleagues who are interested in the project and willing to assist can be invaluable.

Build a Relationship

Establish and maintain a meaningful relationship with your benefactor. Do your best to meet your commitments and execute the plan for which you have been funded. Your benefactor is your ally. Give your total concentration and effort.

Send newspaper clippings about your project with a note to the grantor. Send copies of your school newsletter with articles about the project. Drop the benefactor a note if you are selected to make a presentation about the project at a state conference. Keep the grantor in the communication loop.

If your project involves special events, or if you are honoring project volunteers with a special reception, invite the grantor.

Site Visit

Does your grant provide for the grant-maker to make a site visit? Do you know when that visit will take place? Who from the granting organization will make the visit? Will an auditor be part of the visitor's team and if so, what will she need to see? These are all questions to which you need answers, once you've been told you have the grant.

The site visitors may want to see evidence of

■ Good stewardship of the grant funds,

■ Expenditure records,

■ Compliance with rules and regulations,

- Adherence to evaluation procedures,
- Completion of activities,
- Student progress, and
- Installation and use of equipment purchased with grant funds.

Evaluation

Most grants include some form of evaluation. After you know the terms of the grant, review your commitment to the evaluation procedure. What have you obligated yourself to do? Do you need to collect comments from students, staff, or patrons as a part of formal evaluation? If so, you will need a notebook or a computer file in which to record the comment, that you receive. Could you record video clips of these comments?

Evaluate your project carefully and learn from the process. In addition to collecting data for your formal evaluation report, you may want to informally start collecting quotes from the students, staff, and parents served by the grant. You could use those comments later for feedback to your benefactor, for inclusion in articles and presentations, and possibly in an interim or final report.

You will need a still or video camera to record images of special events and of your project in action. Get film in your camera right away. If you have gotten funding for some type of construction, be sure to take "before," "during," and "after" shots of the project: when the bulldozers raze the old facility and at the ground-breaking ceremony for the new digs.

After the Project

Continue to maintain your relationship with your benefactor. Remind yourself to send an occasional note or clipping to keep in touch and let the funding organization know that the project continues to make an impact.

Extensions

Is it possible to reapply for an additional year of funding for your grant? Many grants are issued for one year, but offer the opportunity to apply for an additional year of funding. Call your grantor and inquire so that you can decide early in the project whether you will be reapplying. It is sometimes easier to get an additional year of funding for your project than it was to get the initial funding.

After regrouping and gathering up your strength, it may be time to start writing a grant for a new project. Take a little time to savor the good feeling of achieving a really difficult goal—writing a winning grant. Then pop open that journal of good ideas and let your imagination help you choose your next project.

In summary, the experience of writing a grant proposal, having it selected for funding, and implementing it is enervating, invigorating, exciting hard work. The more positive an experience you have with winning grant proposals, the more motivated you will be to write more. May the thrill of grant-writing stay fresh for you, and may you succeed in making your school library media center the student-centered, technology-rich learning environment that you picture in your mind.

Appendix A

Selected Works on Grants and Funding

Articles

Bayley, Linda. "Grant Me This: How to Write a Winning Grant Proposal." *School Library Journal* 41 (No. 9 Sept. 1995): 126–128.

Carey, Kelley D. "Renovate or Replace?" *American School Board Journal* (October 2000): 36–37.

Carter, K. "Finding the Funds." *Technology & Learning* 18 (No. 10 June 1998): 6–8+.

___. "Hiring a Grant Writer." *Technology & Learning* 19 (No. 2 September 1998): 72.

Comolli, Tim. "Going After Grants." *electronic school* (January 2001): 32–34.

"Go for the Grant: Creative Classroom's Third Annual Plan-a-Dream Grant. *Creative Classrooms* 13 (No. 2 September/October 1998): 56–57.

Green, D.M. "Targeting That First Research Grant." *ASEE Prism* 8 (No. 1 September 1998): 14.

___. "Writing Your First Grant Proposal." *ASEE Prism* 8 (No 2 October 1998): 14.

Loder, N. "How To Get a Grant." *Times Higher Educational Supplement* 1351 (September 25, 1998): 30.

Vail, Kathleen. "A Piece of History." *American School Board Journal* (October 2000): 38–41.

Ward, Deborah. "Grant Writing Do's and Don'ts." *Technology & Learning* 18 (No. 10 June 1998): 24.

___. "Make the Grant Writing Process a Team Effort." *eSchool News* 3 (No. 3 March 2000): 50.

Whitehead, M. "Digging for Gold." *Times Educational Supplement* 4279 (July 2, 1998): 12.

Wink, D.J. "Proposal Preparation Aids at the NSF Web Site." *Journal of Chemical Education* 75 (No. 8 August 1998): 955.

Books

Barber, Daniel M. *Finding Funding: The Comprehensive Guide to Grant Writing.* Long Beach: Bond Street, 1994.

Barber, Peggy, and Linda D Crowe. *Getting Your Grant: A How-to-Do It Manual for Librarians.* New York: Neal-Schuman, 1993.

Bauer, David G. *The "How To" Grants Manual: Successful Grantseeking Techniques for Obtaining Public and Private Grants.* 4th ed. Phoenix: Orynx, 1999.

___. *The Principal's Guide to Winning Grants.* San Francisco: Jossey-Bass, 1999.

___. *The Teacher's Guide to Winning Grants.* San Francisco: Jossey-Bass, 1999.

Baule, Steven M. *Technology Planning for Effective Teaching and Learning.* 2nd ed. Worthington, Ohio: Linworth Publishing, 2001.

The Big Book of Library Grant Money, 1998 to 1999: Profiles of Private and Corporate Foundations and Direct Corporate Givers Receptive to Library Grant Proposals. Chicago: American Library Association, 1998.

Blum, Laurie. *The Complete Guide to Getting a Grant: How to Turn Your Ideas Into Dollars.* Rev. ed. New York: John Wiley & Sons, 1996.

Brisbois, Matthew W., and Kalte, Pamela M. *The Directory of Corporate and Foundation Givers 2000.* 9th ed. Detroit: The Taft Group, 1999.

Burke, Jim. *I'll Grant You That: A Step-by Step Guide to Finding Funds, Designing Winning Projects, and Writing Powerful Grant Proposals.* Portsmouth, NH: Heinemann, 2000.

Burlingame, Dwight, ed. *Library Fundraising: Models for Success.* Chicago: American Library Association, 1995.

Cantarella, Gina-Marie, ed. *National Guide to Funding for Libraries and Information Services.* 5th ed. New York: Foundation Center, 1999.

Catalog of Federal Domestic Assistance. Washington, D.C.: Office of Management and Budget, 2000.

Corporate 500: The Directory of Corporate Philanthropy. 13th ed. San Francisco: Public Management Institute, 1995.

Cradler, John, and Cordon-Cradler, Ruthmary. *Educator's Guide for Developing and Funding Educational Technology Solutions: A Guidebook for Assisting Educators to Develop and Obtain Funding for Educational Technology Solutions.* 2nd ed. Hillsborough, CA: Educational Support Systems, 1994.

Doggett, Sandra L., and Paula Kay Montgomery. *Beyond the Book: Technology Integration into the Secondary School Library Media Curriculum.* Englewood, CO: Libraries Unlimited, 2000.

An Educator's Guide to Evaluating the Use of Technology in Schools and Classrooms. Washington, D.C.: U.S. Department of Education, Office of Educational Research and Improvement, 1998.

Falkenstein, Jeffrey A., and Melissa Lunn, eds. *The Foundation Directory: Parts 1 and 2*. New York: Foundation Center, 2000.

Falkenstein, Jeffrey A., ed. *National Directory of Corporate Giving*. 6th ed. New York: Foundation Center, 1999.

Ferguson, Jacqueline. *Grants & Awards for Teachers: A Guide to Federal and Private Funding*. 3rd edition. Alexandria, VA: Capitol Publications, 1998.

___. *Grants for Schools: How to Find and Win Funds for K–12 Programs*. 4th ed. Gaithersburg, MD: Aspen, 2000.

___. *The Grantseekers Guide to Project Evaluation*. 2nd ed. Gaithersburg, MD: Aspen, 1999.

Funding Sources for K–12 Education. 2nd ed. Phoenix: Oryx, 1999.

Geever, Jane C., ed. *Foundation Center's Guide to Proposal Writing*. New York: Foundation Center, 2001.

Gelb, Michael J. *How to Think Like Leonardo Da Vinci: Seven Steps to Genius Every Day*. New York: Dell, 2000.

Graham, Christine. *Asking: A Hands-On Learner's Guide to Gift Solicitation*. Shaftsbury, VT: CPG Enterprises, 1998.

___. *Keep the Money Coming: A Step-by-Step Strategic Guide to Annual Fundraising*. Rev. ed. Sarasota: Pineapple, 1992.

Grant$ for Information Technology. New York: Foundation Center, 2000.

Grants for K–12 Schools. Gaithersburg, MD: Aspen, 2000.

Grant$ for Libraries and Information Services. New York: Foundation Center, 2000.

Grants for School Technology: A Guide to Federal and Private Funding. Gaithersburg, MD: Aspen, 1999.

Grants for Schools: Getting Them and Using Them: A Procedural Manual. Malden, MA: Massachusetts Department of Education.

The Grantseeker's Guide to Project Evaluation. 2nd ed. Frederick, MD: Aspen.

Guide to Greater Washington, D.C. Grantmakers. New York: Foundation Center, 1998.

Hackwood, Sara. *Grants Register, 2000*. New York: Saint Martin's Press, 1999.

Hale, Phale D. *GrantWrite: A Step-by-Step System for Writing Grant Proposals That Win*. Alexandria, VA: Capitol, 1997.

___. *Writing Grant Proposals That Win!* 2nd ed. Gaithersburg, MD: Aspen, 2000.

Hoffmann, Frank W., ed. *Grantsmanship for Small Libraries & School Library Media Centers*. Englewood, CO: Libraries Unlimited, 1999.

How to Get Grants and Free Stuff. Annapolis Junction, MD: National Education Association, 1998.

Jacobs, David, and Melissa Lunn, eds. *The Foundation Directory, 2000 Edition, Supplement*. New York: Foundation Center, 2000.

K–12 School Technology Funding Directory. Bethesda, MD: eSchool News Communication Group, 2000.

The K–12 School Technology One Book. Bethesda, MD: eSchool News, 2001.

Kavanaugh, Jennifer, ed. *Education Grants Source Book*. Boston: School Financial Research Center, 1997.

Korenic, Lynette, and Clayton Kirking, eds. *Grant Development for Large and Small Libraries*. Tucson: Art Libraries Society of North America, 1990.

Krebs, Arlene. *The Distance Learning Funding $ourcebook: A Guide to Foundation, Corporate and Government Support for Telecommunications and the New Media*. 4th ed. Dubuque: Kendall/Hunt, 1998.

Lee, Hwa-wei, and Hunt, Gary A. *Fundraising for the 1990s: The Challenge Ahead: A Practical Guide for Library Fundraising, from Novice to Expert*. Canfield, OH: Genaway, 1992.

Lefferts, Robert. *Getting a Grant in the 1990s: How to Write Successful Grant Proposals*. New York: Simon & Schuster, 1992.

MacLean, Rebecca. *The Foundation Grants Index 2001: A Cumulative Listing of Foundation Grants Reported in 1999/2000*. New York: Foundation Center, 2000.

Marshall, Kathleen C., ed. *How to Get More Grant$*. Arlington, VA: Government Information Services, 1994.

Mathis, Emily Duncan, and John Edward Doody. *Grant Proposals: A Primer for Writers*. Washington, D.C.: National Catholic Education Association, 1994.

Mayo, Diane, and Nelson, Sandra. *Wired for the Future: Developing Your Library Technology Plan*. Chicago: American Library Association, 1999.

McConnell, Terry, and Harry W. Sprouse. *Video Production for School Library Media Specialists*. Worthington, OH: Linworth Publishing, 2000.

Miller, Patrick W. *Grant Writing: Strategies for Developing Winning Proposals*. Munster, IN: Patrick W. Miller and Associates, 2000.

Morth, Margaret, ed. *The Foundation Center's User-Friendly Guide, Grantseekers Guide to Resources*. New York: Foundation Center, 1996.

Mudd, Mollie, ed. *Grants for Technology*. Gaithersburg, MD: Aspen, 2001.

New, Cheryl Carter, and Quick, James Aaron. *Grantseekers Toolkit: A Comprehensive Guide to Finding Funding.* New York: J. Wiley, 1998.

Norris, Dennis M. *Get a Grant, Yes You Can!* New York: Scholastic Professional Books, 1998.

Olson, David L. *Grantsmanship: A Primer for School Librarians.* Farmington, ME: University of Maine at Farmington, Mantor Library, 1991.

Orlich, Donald C. *Designing Successful Grant Proposals.* Alexandria, VA: Association for Supervision & Curriculum Development, 1996.

Quiñones, Sherri, and Rita Kirshstein. *An Educator's Guide to Evaluating the Use of Technology in Schools and Classrooms.* Washington, D.C.: U.S. Department of Education Office of Educational Research and Improvement, Educational Resources Information Center, 1999.

Ratzlaff, Leslie A., ed. *Education Grant Winners: Models of Effective Proposal Structure and Style.* Alexandria, VA: Capitol, 1991.

Rich, Elizabeth H., ed. *National Guide to Funding for Libraries and Information Services.* New York: Foundation Center, 1997.

Ruskin, Karen B., and Charles M. Achilles. *Grantwriting, Fundraising, and Partnerships: Strategies That Work!* Thousand Oaks, CA: Corwin, 1995.

Schrock, Kathleen, ed. *The Technology Connection: Building a Successful Library Media Program.* Worthington, OH: Linworth Publishing, 2000.

A Teacher's Guide to Fellowships and Awards. Maiden, MA: Massachusetts Department of Education, 1995.

Technology Innovation Challenge Grants. Washington, D.C.: U.S. Department of Education, Office of Educational Research and Improvement, 2001.

What Should I Know About ED Grants? 2nd ed. Washington, D.C.: Office of the Chief Financial Officer, U.S. Department of Education. Office of Educational Research and Improvement, 1998.

Whole Nonprofit Catalog: A Compendium of Sources and Resources for Managers and Staff of Nonprofit Organizations. Los Angeles: Grantsmanship Center, 1984.

Winer, Michael Barry, and Karen Louise Ray. *Collaboration Handbook: Creating, Sustaining and Enjoying the Journey.* St. Paul: Amherst H. Wilder Foundation, 1994.

Journals

Cable in the Classroom, 1800 N. Beauregard St., Suite 100, Alexandria, VA 22311. 800-743-5355.

The Chronicle of Philanthropy. Chronicle of Philanthropy, 1225 23rd Street, NW, Washington, D.C. 20037.

Computer.Grants.Alert. Aspen Publishers, 7201 McKinney Circle, Frederick, MD 21701.

Corporate Giving Watch. Taft Group, 835 Penobscot Bldg., Detroit, MI 48226.

Corporate Philanthropy Report. Capitol Publications, 1101 King St., Suite 444, Alexandria, VA 22314.

Curriculum Administrator. Educational Media, 488 Main Ave., Norwalk, CT 06851. 203-847-7200.

Education Grants Alert. Aspen Publishers, 7201 McKinney Circle, Frederick, MD 21701.

Educational Technology. Educational Technology Publications, 700 Palisade Ave., Englewood Cliffs, NJ 07632-0564. 800-952-2665.

eSchool News. eSchool News Communications Group, 7920 Norfolk Ave., Suite 900, Bethesda, MD 20814. 800-394-0115.

Foundation Giving Watch. Taft Group, 835 Penobscot Bldg., Detroit, MI 48226.

Foundation News. Council on Foundations, 1828 L Street NW, Suite 300, Washington, D.C. 20036.

Grants Magazine. Plenum Publishing, 233 Spring St., New York, NY 10013.

Learning and Leading with Technology. International Society for Technology in Education, 480 Charnelton St, Eugene, OR 97401-2626. 800-336-5191.

Media & Methods. American Society of Educators, 1429 Walnut St., Philadelphia, PA 19102. 800-555-5657.

Technology and Learning. Miller Freeman, 600 Harrison St., San Francisco, CA 94107. 415-947-6746.

T.H.E. Journal. T.H.E. Journa, 17501 17th St., Suite 230, Tustin, CA 92780. 714-730-4011.

Online Journals

Curriculum Administrator Online. <www.educatorsportal.com>

Electronic School. <http://www.electronic-school.com>

Eschool News online. <www.eschoolnews.com/>

From Now On: The Educational Technology Journal. <www.fno.org>

ISTE's Learning & Leading With Technology. <www.iste.org>

Media & Methods Magazine. <www.media-methods.com>

T.H.E. Journal Online. <www.thejournal.com>

TechLEARNING. <www.techlearning.com>

Web Sites

American Memory Fellows Program. <http://learning.loc.gov/learn/amfp>

AOL Foundation. <http://www.aolfoundaton.org>

Bell Atlantic Foundation Grants. <http://www.bellatlanticfoundation.com>

Benton Foundation. <http://www.benton.org/>

Brinker International Charitable Committee. <www.brinker.com/htm/006_company info_framesource_communityrelations.htm>

Carnegie Corporation of New York. <http://www.carnegie.org/>

Catalog of Federal Domestic Assistance. <http://www.cfda.gov>

Challenge Grants for Technology in Education. <http://www.ed.gov/Technology/chalgrnt.html>

The Chronicle of Philanthropy. <http://philanthropy.com/>

Community of Science. <http://www.cos.com/>

Compaq's Teaching with Technology Grant Program. <http://www.compaq.com/education/k12/success/devgrant_2000.html>

Converge Magazine—Grants Page. <http://www.convergemag.com/grants.shtm>

Cooperative State Research, Education, and Extension Service of USDA (CSREES). <http://www.reeusda.gov/1700/funding/ourfund.htm>

Council for the Advancement and Support of Education. <http://www.case.org/>

Council on Foundations. <http://www.cof.org/home.htm>

Curricular Resources & Networking Projects. <http://www.ed.gov/EdRes/EdCurric.html>

Department of Computer Science, University of Virginia. <http://www.cs.virginia.edu/research/sponsors.html>

Department of Education's Technology Innovation Challenge Grants. <http://www.ed.gov/Technology/challenge/>

Distance Learning Funding Sourcebook. <http://www.technogrants.com>

Dow Chemical Company Foundation Grants. <http://www.dow.com/about/corp/social/social.htm>

J.C. Downing Foundation. <http://www.jcdowning.org/>

Edsitement. <http://edsitement.neh.gov/>

Ed-Tech Alert. <http://www.edtech-alert.com>

Education Programs. (Searchable database of 200+ programs administered by U.S. Dept. of Education). <http://inet.ed.gov/cgi-bin/wwwwais_edp>

Education World © Grants for Educators Program.
    <www.educationworld.com/grants/>

Educational Funding Strategies. <http://www.icu.com/efs/home.htm>

Educational Grant Sponsors Index.
    <http://www.cs.virginia.edu/~seas/resdev/sponsors.html>

Educational Renaissance Grant Information.
    <http://www.anovember.com/grants.html>

The Electric Newsstand. <http://www.enews.com>

eSchool News Online—School Technology Funding Center.
    <www.eschoolnews.com/funding>

Federal Register. <http://www.access.gpo.gov/#info>

___. U.S. Department of Education Documents.
    <http://www.ed.gov/legislation/FedRegister/announcements/index.html>

Federal Resources for Educational Excellence.
    <http://www.ed.gov:80/free/981210.html>

Foundation Center. <http://fdncenter.org/>

Foundations On-line. <http://www.foundations.org>

Fulbright Scholar Program. <http://www.iie.org/ceis/>

Funding for Technology. <http://www.mcrel.org/resources/technology/funding.asp>

FundsNet Online Services. <http://www.fundsnetservices.com/>

FY 1999–2001 Discretionary Grant Application Packages.
    <http://www.ed.gov/GrantApps/>

George Lucas Educational Foundation. <http://glef.org/>

Government Nonprofit Gateway. <http://www.nonprofit.gov/resource/>

Grant and Funding Resources for K–12 Education Homepage.
    <http://www.ospi.wednet.edu/grants.html>

Grant Hotline (Quinlan Publishing). <http://www.quinlan.com/gdc/index.html>

Grant Proposal Writing. <http://www.wilbers.com/grants.htm>

Grant Seeker's Guide. <http://www.nonprofit.net/info/guide.html>

Grantmakers for Education. <http://www.edfunders.org/>

Grants and Contests Search. <http://www.techlearning.com/grants.shtml>

Grants and Funding Center at eSchoolNews.com.
    <http://www.eschoolnews.com/grants/main.html>

Grants & Funding for School Technology. <http://www.eschoolnews.com/gf>

Grants and Other People's Money (NASA).
<http://quest.arc.nasa.gov/top/grants.html>

Grants and Related Resources, Michigan State University.
<http://www.lib.msu.edu/harris23/grants/>

Grants for Nonprofits: Children and Youth.
<www.lib.msu.edu/harris23/grants/2child.htm>

Grantsmanship Center. <http://www.tgci.com/>

GrantSmart. <http://www.grantsmart.org/index.html>

GrantsWeb. <http://srainternational.org/cws/sra/resource.htm>

Grantwriters.com. <www.grantwriters.com>

Henry Moore Foundation. <http://www.henry-moore-fdn.co.uk/hmf/>

Institute of Museum and Library Services.
<www.imls.gov/grants/library/nlgl_rec.asp>

Intel Foundation Grants. <http://www.intel.com/intel/community/grants.htm>

Interactive Education Initiative, AOL Foundation. e-mail: AOLGrants@AOL.com

Internet Nonprofit Center. <http://nonprofits.org>

The Internet Prospector. <http://w3.uwyo.edu/~prospect/>

Jay Mendell's Links to Grants Information on the Internet.
<http://House-of-Hope.org/grants-central-station.htm>

JDL Technologies. <http://www.jdltech.com>

Kathy Schrock's Guide for Educators.
<http://school.discovery.com/schrockguide/business/grants.html>

LTP Education Resources. <learn.arc.nasa.gov/grants/grants.html>

Media and Methods. <http://www.media-methods.com>

Michael Jordan Fundamentals Education Grants Program for Teachers, National
Foundation for the Improvement of Education. <www.nfie.org>

Microsoft's Grant Information Page.
<http://www.microsoft.com/Education/students/grant.asp>

MultiMedia Schools. <http://www.infotoday.com/MMSchools>

NASA K12 Internet Initiative: Grant Info.
<http://quest.arc.nasa.gov/top/grants.html>

National Charities Information Bureau. <http://www.give.org/>

National Endowment for the Arts. <http://arts.endow.gov/>

National Endowment for the Humanities. <http://www.neh.fed.us/>

National Science Foundation. <http://www.nsf.gov/home/grants.htm>

NCSS Online. <http://www.ncss.org/home.html>

Nonprofit Resources Catalogue. <http://www.clark.net/pub/pwalker/>

Nonprofit Universe/GrantScape. <http://www.nonprofituniverse.com/>

Philanthropy News Digest. <http://fdncenter.org/phil/philmain.html>

Philanthropy News Network Online. <http://pnnonline.org/>

Philanthropy News Network Online (e-rate).
        <http://pnnonline.org/education/erate0417.cfm>

Pitsco's Launch to Grants and Funding. <http://www.pitsco.com/p/grants.html>

Polaris. <www.polarisgrantscentral.net>

Preparing Tomorrow's Teachers to Use Technology. <http://www.ed.gov/teachtech>

Resource Pages for Educational Grantseekers.
        <http://www.col-ed.org/fund/fund.html>

Resources Guide to Federal Funding for Technology in Education.
        <http://www.ed.gov/Technology/tec-guid.html>

Robert H. Michel Civic Education Grants.
        <http://www.pekin.net/dirksen/micheledgrants.html>

SAMI, Science and Math Initiatives. <http://www.learner.org/sami/>

Sample Grant Proposal.
        <http://teacher.scholastic.com/professional/grants/sampropo.htm>

Scholastic Network. <http://.teacher.scholastic.com/professional/grants/index.htm>

School Planning and Management. <http://www.spmmag.com>

SchoolGrants. <http://www.schoolgrants.org>

SchoolPop.com. <http://www.schoolpop.com>

Schools and Libraries Division of USAC. <http://www.sl.universalservice.org>

School-to-Work. <http://stw.ed.gov/>

Study Web's Foundations & Grants Links.
        <http://www.studyWeb.com/educate/found.htm>

TGCI (The Grantsmanship Center). <http://www.tgci.com>

Target Teacher Scholarships. <http://target.com/schools/scholarships.asp>

Teacher Universe. <http://www.teacheruniverse.com>

The Teachers Network–Impact II.
        <www.teachnet.org/docs/Funders/Welcome/index.htm>

Tech.LEARNING Grants & Contests. <http://www.techlearning.com/grants.html>

Technology & Learning Online—Grants and Contests.
<http://www.techlearning.com/grants.shtml>

Telecommunications and Information Infrastructure Assistance Program.
<http://www.ntia.doc.gov/otiahome/tiiap/index.html>

Toshiba America Foundation. <www.toshiba.com>

Training Grants from Inspiration Software. <http://www.inspiration.com >

21st Century Community Learning Centers. <http:/www.ed.gov/21stcclc>

U.S. Department of Education. <http://www.ed.gov/>

___, Funding. <http://www.ed.gov/funding.html>

___, Grants and Contracts Information. <http://ocfo.ed.gov/>

___, Grants and Contracts. <http://gcs.ed.gov/>

___, Office of Postsecondary Education, Higher Education Programs.
<http://www.ed.gov/offices/OPE/OHEP/solicit.html>

U.S. Government and Grant Resources. <http://psyche.uthct.edu/ous/Govt.html>

University of Illinois at Chicago Office of the Vice Chancellor for Research.
<http://www.uic.edu/depts/ovcr/>

Online Grant-Writing Help

DOE and Westinghouse Technology Transfer and Economic Development
Program. <http://www.t2ed.com/>

The Foundation Center's Online Library. <http://fdncenter.org/onlib/index.html>

Grant Guides Plus—Grantseeker.com. <http://www.grantseeker.com/strategy.htm>

The Grantseeking Process—Online Orientation by the Foundation Center.
<http://fdncenter.org/onlib/orient/intro1.html>

A Proposal Writing Short Course, Foundation Center.
<http://fdncenter.org/onlib/shortcourse/prop1.html>

The User-Friendly Guide to Funding Research and Resources.
<http://fdncenter.org/onlib/ufg/index.html>

Funding Sources

National Network of Grantmakers
2335 18th Street NW
Washington, D.C. 20009
202-483-0030

National Society of Fund-Raising Executives
1101 King St., Suite 3000
Alexandria, VA 22314
703-684-0410

Office of Publications and Public Affairs
National Endowment for the Humanities
1100 Pennsylvania Ave. NW
Washington, D.C. 20506
202-786-0438

U.S. Department of Education Library Programs
Office of Educational Research and Improvement (OERI)
555 New Jersey Ave.
Washington, D.C. 20208-5571
202-219-1315
Fax: 202-219-1466

Appendix B

U.S. Department of Education Technology Programs

Capacity-Building

Technology Literacy Challenge Fund provides funding to help states and school districts develop and implement plans to meet the four national educational technology goals. 202-401-0039 or <http://www.ed.gov/Technology/TLCF/>.

Community Networks

Community Technology Centers expand access to technology centers in low-income communities. 202-205-8270 or <http://www.ed.gov/offices/OVAE/CTC/>.

Distance Learning

Star Schools supports project that utilize distance learning technology to provide instructional programs to students and professional development to teachers in underserved populations. 202-219-2186 or <http://www.ed.gov/prog_info/StarSchools/index.html>.

Learning Anytime Anywhere Partnerships support partnerships of colleges, universities, businesses, community organizations, or other entities that deliver quality postsecondary distance education. 202-708-5750 or <http://www.ed.gov/offices/OPE/FIPSE/learnany.html>.

Innovation

Technology Innovation Challenge Grants promote innovative uses of educational technology by awarding grants to partnerships of school districts, universities, businesses, libraries, software designers, and others. 202-208-3882 or <http://www.ed.gov/Technology/challenge/>.

Professional Development

Preparing Tomorrow's Teachers to Use Technology helps ensure that tomorrow's teachers are prepared to integrate technology effectively into the curriculum and to use the new teaching and learning styles enabled by technology. 202-260-1365 or <www.ed.gov/teachtech/>.

Research

Interagency Education Research Initiative is an initiative of the U.S. Department of Education, National Science Foundation, and National Institutes of Health to focus expertise in research, evaluation, and educational technology on achieving two important educational goals: Ensuring that all children acquire the foundations of mathematics and reading by the end of grade three, and ensuring that all mathematics, science, and reading teachers have high-level content in these areas. 202-219-1935 or <http://www.ehr.nsf.gov/eri-ed-nsf/>.

Technical Assistance

Regional Technology in Education Consortia's six centers provide states, school districts, adult literacy programs, and other education institutions with professional development, technical assistance, and information about the use of advanced technologies to improve teaching and learning. 202-219-8070 or <http://rtec.org/>.

Other Federal Resources

Federal Communications Commission oversees the E-Rate (Education Rate), which provides affordable access to advanced telecommunications services for all schools and libraries in the United States. Contact the Schools and Libraries Division at 202-776-0200 or go to <http://www.sl.universalservice.org/>.

Federal Resources for Educational Excellence is an Internet tool for teaching and learning, developed by more than 30 federal agencies, which makes hundreds of federally supported education resources available at <http://www.ed.gov/free/what.html>.

Department of Commerce Telecommunications and Information Infrastructure Application Program (TIIAP) supports planning and construction of telecommunications. Contact TIIAP at 202-482-2048 or go to <http://www.ntia.doc.gov/otiahome/otiahome.html>.

National Science Foundation makes grants and awards in all areas of science, mathematics, and engineering education. Contact NSF at 703-306-1234 or go to <http://www.nsf.gov/home/her>.

Department of Energy's 10 national laboratories and 30 technology centers and research facilities provide educational experiences for students, training and curriculum materials for preservice and inservice teachers, and literacy programs for the general public. DOE also runs Computers for Learning, which will place hundreds of thousands of surplus government computers in U.S. classrooms. Contact Computers for Learning at 888-362-7870 or go to <http://www.computers.fed.gov>.

National Aeronautics and Space Administration: NASA provides online educational programs and services. Visit <http://www.education.nasa.gov>.

U.S. Department of Agriculture's Distance Learning and Telemedicine grants support telemedicine services and distance learning services in rural areas. Contact the Rural Utilities Service at 202-720-4581 or go to <http://www.usda.gov/rus/dlt/1703.pdf>.

The U.S. Department of Education's Office of Educational Technology (OET) develops national educational technology policy and coordinates and implements this policy through its programs. Working closely with the offices of Elementary and Secondary Education (OESE), Educational Research and Improvement (OERI), Postsecondary Education (OPE), Vocational and Adult Education (OVAE), and Special Education and Rehabilitative Services (OSERS), OET helps to ensure that these programs are also coordinated with efforts across the federal government. A primary focus of OET's work is evaluating the effectiveness of educational technology. OET's leadership priorities currently include

- Promoting equal access to technology,
- Ensuring Internet safety,
- Encouraging new strategies for software development, and
- Planning the nation's long-term policy for educational technology.

Educational Technology publications are available at <http://www.ed.gov/Technology/> or by calling 877-4ED-PUBS or 800-USA-LEARN.

The most requested publications include

- *Getting America's Students Ready for the 21st Century: Meeting the Technology Literacy Challenge,*
- *Parents' Guide to the Internet,*
- *An Educator's Guide to Evaluating the Use of Technology in Schools and Classrooms, and*
- *Distance Education in Higher Education Institutions.*

Government Technology Grant Sources

Technology Literacy Challenge Fund grants support the development and implementation of systemic technology plans at the state, local, and school levels to improve the teaching and learning of all children. Contact Thomas Fagan 202-401-0039, e-mail *Thomas_Fagan@ed.gov* for more information.

Technology, Educational Media, and Materials for Individuals with Disabilities is a program whose purpose is to advance the availability, quality, use, and effectiveness of technology, education media, and materials in the education of children and youth with disabilities. It also provides for early intervention services to infants and toddlers with disabilities. Contact Jane Hauser 202-205-8126, e-mail *Jane_Hauser@ed.gov*.

National Educational Technology Goals

1. All teachers and students will have modern computers in their classrooms,

2. Every classroom will be connected to the information superhighway,

3. All teachers in the nation will have the training and support they need to help all students learn through computers and the information super highway, and

4. Effective and engaging software and online resources will be an integral part of every school curriculum.

U.S. Department of Education
Office of Educational Technology
400 Maryland Ave. SW
Suite 6W301
Washington, D.C. 20202
Phone: 202-401-1444
Fax: 202-401-3941
Web site: <http://www.ed.gov/Technology/>
(This information taken from brochure entitled *Educational Technology Programs at the U.S. Department of Education.*)

Appendix C

Glossary

Abstract. A cogent summary of a proposed project; a quick overview, usually one page, used to persuade the reader to read the proposal and the grantor to fund it.

Acronyms. Words formed by the initial letters of a name or series of words. Example: ED is Education Department.

Activities. Events planned to accomplish the goals of a project.

Analog. A system that relies on computer-based reproduction of sound and image.

Annual report. An account of the achievements and financial information of an organization for the past year, which usually includes a sponsor's goals and mission.

Appendixes. Attachments to a grant proposal. They may include resumes, organizational charts, agency publications, letters of support, reprints of articles, other supporting data.

Applicant. Person or organization seeking grant funding.

Application notice. A government notice published in the *Federal Register* that invites applications for one or more discretionary grant or cooperative agreement competitions, gives basic program and fiscal information on each competition, informs potential applicants when and where they can obtain applications, and cites the deadline for applying.*

Application package. Package containing the application notice for one or more programs, and all the information and forms needed to apply for a discretionary grant.*

Appropriations legislation. A law passed by the Congress to provide a certain level of funding for a grant program in a given year.*

Authorizing agent. The person appointed by the school board to sign legal documents.

Authorizing legislation. A law passed by the Congress that establishes or continues a grant program.*

Award. A grant.

*Definitions provided by the U.S. Department of Education publication *What Should I Know About ED Grants?*

Award notice. Formal notification from grantor to applicant announcing award of a grant.

Baseline data. Evaluation data demonstrating the status prior to implementation of the grant project.

Benchmarks. Interim reference points during a grant project that indicate progress.

Block grant. A type of government grant issued to another unit of government for dispersal determined by a formula.

Budget period. An interval of time into which a project period is divided for budgetary purposes, usually 12 months.*

Capital outlay. Furniture, equipment, and hardware, such as computers, tables, and projectors.

***Catalog of Federal Domestic Assistance* (CFDA).** Publication and database produced by the General Services Administration that lists the domestic assistance programs of all federal agencies with information about authorization, fiscal details, accomplishments, regulations, guidelines, eligibility requirements, information contacts, and application and award process.*

Coalition. A group of interested parties or organizations who come together for a special purpose.

Competitive review process. The process used by the Department of Education to evaluate grant proposals and cooperative agreement applications, in which applications are scored by subject-area experts, and those with highest scores considered for funding.*

Consortium. A group of organizations who join together to submit a grant application.

Construction grant. Money awarded for building or renovating facilities.

Continuation application. A request to continue funding for an existing project for an additional time period.

Continuation grant. Additional funding awarded for budget periods following the initial budget period of a multi-year grant.*

Cost Sharing. Costs that a school or district will contribute to the project. They can be "in-kind" costs, such as the use of space or volunteers, as well as actual cash outlay.

*Definitions provided by the U.S. Department of Education publication *What Should I Know About ED Grants?*

Criteria. Characteristics on which a proposal will be evaluated.

Curriculum vita. Resume, brief summary of one's education, professional history, and job qualifications.

Deadline. The date by which an applicant must mail a grant application for it to be considered for funding. In some competitions, the grantor requires that the application be received by the deadline date, not just mailed by that date.*

Demographic data. Statistical or factual information about a target group or community.

Digital. A system that measures physical changes in variable qualities, such as sound waves.

Direct assistance. A grant that provides personnel, equipment, or supplies, not money.

Direct costs. Line items explicitly listed in the budget as expenditures.

Discretionary grant. An award of financial assistance in the form of money, or property in lieu of money, by the federal government to an eligible grantee, usually made on the basis of a competitive review process.*

Dissemination. The means by which information is given to others about a project. Usually includes purpose, methods, and accomplishments of the project. May be a section of a grant proposal.

E-Rate. A federal fund to help schools and libraries gain Internet access at a reasonable price.

ED. The acronym for the U.S. Department of Education.*

Employee benefits. Fringe benefits, such as health insurance.

Evaluation. The manner in which a project's impact on students or participants will be measured.

Executive summary. An abstract; the concise description of a project; a section of a grant proposal.

Federal Register. A daily compilation of federal regulations and legal notices, presidential proclamations and executive orders, federal agency documents having general applicability and legal effect, documents required to be published by act of Congress, and other federal agency documents of public interest; prepared by the National Archives and Records Administration for public distribution by the Government Printing Office; publication of record for ED regulations.*

*Definitions provided by the U.S. Department of Education publication *What Should I Know About ED Grants?*

Fiscal year. A 12-month period for budget purposes.

Formative evaluation. A type of project evaluation designed to provide immediate feedback. It assesses procedures used and progress being made.

Formula grant. A grant that the Department of Education is directed by Congress to make to grantees, for which the amount is established by a formula based on certain criteria that are written into the legislation and program regulations; directly awarded and administered in the Department of Education's program offices.*

Fringe benefits. Amounts paid by an employer for retirement, heath insurance, and other employee benefits.

Full-time equivalent (FTE). A weighted formula that accounts for part-time, special needs, non-English-speaking, and other categories of students in terms of full-time enrollment.

Funding offer. A Department of Education proposal, either oral or written, that an applicant accept a level of funding less than the applicant's request. This occurs when the Department either does not accept certain items of cost in the applicant's original budget or does not have sufficient money to fund all recommended projects at the requested level.*

Goals. Purpose of a project.

Government grant. Funding from the federal, state, or local government.

Grant. Financial assistance given for a specific purpose and time period as outlined in an application or proposal.

Grant application reviewer (reviewer). An individual who serves the Department of Education by reviewing new discretionary grant applications; also referred to as 'field reader' or 'peer reviewer.'*

Grant Award Notification (GAN). Official document signed by an authorized official stating the amount, terms, and conditions of an award for a discretionary grant or cooperative agreement from the Department of Education.*

Grant closeout. The final phase in the life cycle of a discretionary grant during which the Department of Education ensures that the grantee has met the requirements of a grant and makes final fiscal adjustments to a grantee's account.*

Grantee. The person or group of people receiving a grant.

Grantor. The entity making the grant funds available.

*Definitions provided by the U.S. Department of Education publication *What Should I Know About ED Grants?*

Grants Management Officer. Someone on the grantor's staff who oversees dispersal of grant funds.

Guidelines. Rules, regulations, and specifications to be followed in applying for a grant.

Higher Education Programs (HEP). A section of the U.S. Education Department.

Indirect costs. Costs incurred for common or joint objectives that cannot be readily and specifically identified with a particular grant project or other institutional activity.* Costs not explicitly listed in the budget as a line item. Private foundations usually refer to indirect costs as *administrative costs*. Corporations may call the same costs *overhead*.

In-kind support. Grantee's non-cash contributions to a grant project.

Letter of intent. A letter to a grantor briefly describing a project and requesting permission to apply for a grant.

Letter of support or commitment. A letter from a supervisor, expert, or stakeholder to a grantor vouching for an applicant's credentials and a project's potential success.

Local education agency (LEA). The school district or educational service agency that will receive and disburse the grant funds.

Matching funds. Money or in-kind services a grantor requires a recipient to contribute.

Mission. An organization's chief function or responsibility.

Monitoring. Activities undertaken by Education Department staff members to review and evaluate specific aspects of a grantee's activities under a discretionary grant; they include

- Measuring a grantee's performance,
- Assessing a grantee's adherence to applicable laws, regulations, and terms and conditions of the award,
- Providing technical assistance, and
- Assessing whether a grantee has made substantial progress.*

Needs statement. The section of the proposal that describes the need for the project. It usually contains meaningful statistics and educational research.

*Definitions provided by the U.S. Department of Education publication *What Should I Know About ED Grants?*

Notice of grant award. The formal notification from the grantor describing the grant amount, requirements, and time periods.

Objectives. Measurable statements or outcomes that demonstrate changes or growth resulting from a project.

Oversight committee. An advisory group charged with overseeing the administration of a grant.

Partnership. An alliance formed between individuals or groups in order to participate in a mutually advantageous project.

Per diem. The cost per day for the travel expenses, hotel, and meals.

Performance report. A report of the specific activities the grant recipient has performed during the budget or project period.*

Personal digital assistant. Handheld electronic device for computing and data storage and retrieval.

Post-award performance conference. The first major discussion between the Department of Education and some grantees after a new award has been made, generally focusing on the proposed project outcomes as stated in the grantee's approved application, and on the ways in which progress will be assessed.*

Program announcement. Notification in the Federal Register describing an opportunity to apply for a grant.

Program officer. The person who supervises grant funds for a philanthropic organization and explains program guidelines and the benefactor's mission to applicants.

Program regulations. Regulations that implement legislation passed by Congress to authorize a specific grant program; they include

- Applicant and participant eligibility criteria,
- Nature of activities funded,
- Costs allowed,
- Selection criteria, and
- Other relevant information.*

Project officer. See *Program officer*

Project period. The total amount of time (sometimes several years) during which the grantor authorizes a grantee to complete the project described in the application. Project periods of more than one year are divided into budget periods. Sometimes referred to as 'performance period.'*

*Definitions provided by the U.S. Department of Education publication *What Should I Know About ED Grants?*

Proposal. A written document of detailed information about a proposed project that an applicant submits to a grantor.

Proposal letter. A preliminary proposal sent in the form of a letter.

Query Letter. A letter sent to a potential grantor outlining a broad overview of the project proposal. The grantee is exploring the funding source's interest in the project before submitting a formal proposal.

Request for proposal (RFP) or request for application (RFA). A grantor's request for submissions; usually includes guidelines and necessary forms.

Rubric. A form, provided by the grantor, used for scoring a grant proposal. The rubric may or may not be included in the guidelines.

Sponsor. The grantor.

Staff Development. Continuing education opportunity for staff involved in the grant project.

Stakeholders. The people in an organization who will participate in or benefit from a grant project.

Statement of purpose. A section of the proposal describing the intended results anticipated from the implementation of a project.

Stipend. A payment provided for participation in or service to a project.

Substantial progress. A level of achievement that a grantee must make in its project during a specified period of time (e.g., budget period, performance period), which produces measurable and verifiable evidence that the activities undertaken have attained a preponderance of project goals and objectives during the period.*

Summation evaluation. The final evaluation of a project's results.

Time line. A graph or narrative explaining which tasks are to be accomplished, by whom, over which time periods.

Unsolicited proposal. A proposal sent without the grantor's request.

Video streaming. A method of delivering motion video with audio live through the Internet. The user does not have to download a file to a computer and then play it back.

Vision. The plan envisioned for the future of a project or organization.

*Definitions provided by the U.S. Department of Education publication *What Should I Know About ED Grants?*

Appendix D

U.S. Department of Education Grant and Contract Forms

Important Notice to Prospective Participants in U.S. Department of Education Contract and Grant Programs

---

Grants

Applicants for grants from the U.S. Department of Education (ED) have to compete for limited funds.

Deadlines assure all applicants that they will be treated fairly and equally, without last minute haste.

For these reasons, ED must set strict deadlines for grant applications. Prospective applicants can avoid disappointment if they understand that:

> Failure to meet a deadline will mean that an applicant will be Rejected without any consideration whatever.

The rules, including the deadline, for applying for each grant are published, individually, in the Federal Register. A one-year subscription to the Register may be obtained by sending $340.00 to: Superintendent of Documents, U.S. Government Printing Office, Washington, D.C. 20402-9371. (Send check or money order only, no cash or stamps.)

The instructions in the Federal Register must be followed exactly. Do not accept any other advice you may receive. No ED employee is authorized to extend any deadline published in the Register.

Questions regarding submission of applications may be addressed to:

U.S. Department of Education
Application Control Center
Washington, D.C. 20202-4725

Contracts

Competitive procurement actions undertaken by the ED are governed by the Federal Procurement Regulation and implementing ED Procurement Regulation.

Generally, prospective competitive procurement actions are synopsized in the Commerce Business Daily (CBD). Prospective offerors are therein advised of the nature of the procurement and where to apply for copies of the Request for Proposals (RFP).

Offerors are advised to be guided solely by the contents of the CBD synopsis and the instructions contained in the RFP. Questions regarding the submission of offers should be addressed to the Contracts Specialist identified on the face page of the RFP.

Offers are judged in competition with others, and failure to conform with any substantive requirements of the RFP will result in rejection of the offer without any consideration whatever.

Do not accept any advice you receive that is contrary to instructions contained in either the CBD synopsis or the RFP. No ED employee is authorized to consider a proposal which is non-responsive to the RFP.

A subscription to the CBD is available for $208 per year via second class mailing or $261.00 per year via first class mailing. Information included in the Federal Acquisition Regulation is contained in Title 48, Code of Federal Regulations, Chapter 1 ($49.00). The foregoing publication may be obtained by sending your check or money order only, no cash or stamps, to:

Superintendent of Documents
U.S. Government Printing Office
Washington, D.C. 20402-9371

In an effort to be certain this important information is widely disseminated, this notice is being included in all ED mail to the public. You may therefore, receive more than one notice. If you do, we apologize for any annoyance it may cause you.

ED FORM 5348, 8/92
REPLACES ED FORM 5348, 6/86 WHICH IS OBSOLETE

Appendix E

Top 10 U.S. Foundations by Total Giving

The list below includes the 10 largest U.S. grant-making foundations ranked by total giving, based on the most current audited financial data in the Foundation Center's database as of June 28, 2000. Total giving figures include grants, scholarships, employee matching gifts, and other amounts reported as "grants and contributions paid during the year" on the 990-PF tax form. Total giving does not include all qualifying distributions under the tax law, e.g., loans, program-related investments, and program or other administrative expenses.

Rank	Name/(state)	Total Giving	As of Fiscal Year End Date
1.	Lilly Endowment Inc. (IN)	$557,301,037	12/31/99
2.	The Ford Foundation (NY)	511,825,000	09/30/99
3.	The Robert Wood Johnson Foundation (NJ)	288,126,426	12/31/98
4.	The David and Lucile Packard Foundation (CA)	263,929,118	12/31/98
5.	W.K. Kellogg Foundation (MI)	202,919,594	08/31/99
6.	Robert W. Woodruff Foundation, Inc. (GA)	191,355,356	12/31/99
7.	The Pew Charitable Trusts (PA)	161,411,658	12/31/98
8.	The Rockefeller Foundation (NY)	149,343,068	12/31/99
9.	The Andrew W. Mellon Foundation (NY)	142,216,007	12/31/98
10.	The New York Community Trust (NY)	130,680,652	12/31/99

Source: Foundation Center

Appendix F

Sample Grant Proposal Format

(Hypothetical)

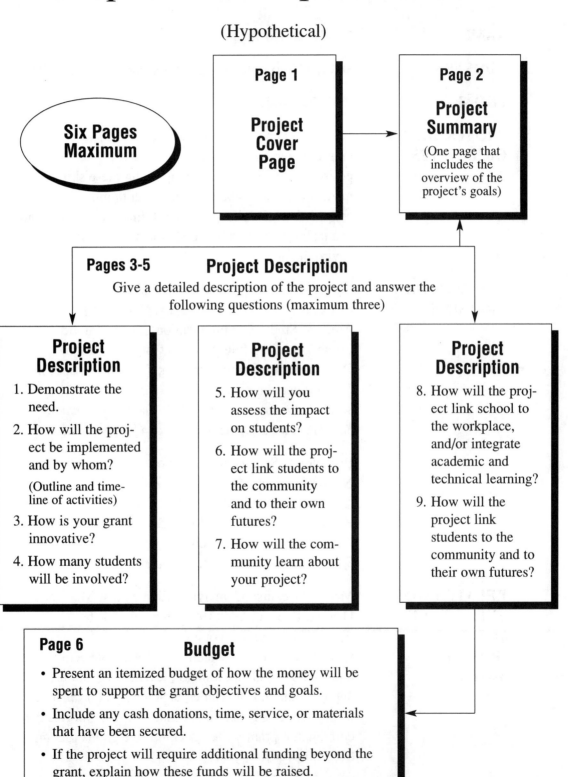

Six Pages Maximum

Page 1

Project Cover Page

Page 2

Project Summary

(One page that includes the overview of the project's goals)

Pages 3-5　　**Project Description**

Give a detailed description of the project and answer the following questions (maximum three)

Project Description

1. Demonstrate the need.

2. How will the project be implemented and by whom?

   (Outline and time-line of activities)

3. How is your grant innovative?

4. How many students will be involved?

Project Description

5. How will you assess the impact on students?

6. How will the project link students to the community and to their own futures?

7. How will the community learn about your project?

Project Description

8. How will the project link school to the workplace, and/or integrate academic and technical learning?

9. How will the project link students to the community and to their own futures?

Page 6　　**Budget**

- Present an itemized budget of how the money will be spent to support the grant objectives and goals.

- Include any cash donations, time, service, or materials that have been secured.

- If the project will require additional funding beyond the grant, explain how these funds will be raised.

Appendix G

Sample Resume

NAME	Carolyn S. Hoffman
ADDRESS	888 E. Clinton Street, Apt. 2089, Phoenix, AZ 85020
PHONE	(602) 298-4447
PROFESSIONAL OBJECTIVES	My professional objectives are to implement past and present teaching experience in a global leadership position. I feel competent in applying these skills in media (video and library science), communications, community relations, personnel training and development and technology; both in education and in corporate environments.
EDUCATIONAL TRAINING	Master of Arts Degree in Communication Bowling Green State University, OH (1975) Areas of Study: Communication Theory, Public Communication, Interpersonal Communication, Organizational Communication, Teaching of Speech Communication. Thesis: *Investigation and Assessment of the Communication Needs of the Navajo Indian Student in a Fundamental Speech Communication Course*
	Bachelor of Science in Education Northern Arizona University, AZ (1974) Areas of Study: Small-Group Communication, Debate, Public Communication, Mass Communication, Theatre, Library Science (Minor emphasis) *Arizona Certification in Speech, Drama, Library Science K–12*
RELATED WORK EXPERIENCE *Media and Technology Specialist*	<u>Media Specialist</u>, Camelview Elementary, Madison School District, Phoenix, AZ (1997-Present). Teacher of library skills, on line computer research information specialist, Internet research and global connections facilitator, school Web coordinator, teacher of literature appreciation and storyteller, technology coordinator, Young Authors Program coordinator, Artist in Residence coordinator, grant writer (secured five grants totaling $18,000 over four years).

Media and
Technology
Specialist cont.

Supervisor of Media Services, Cartwright School District, Phoenix, AZ (1995-1997). Coordinator of thirteen elementary school libraries and three middle school media centers. Responsible for acquisition and processing of book and media resources; staff development in using literature; and providing strategies on how to integrate library resources with classroom instruction in the areas of reference, research and study skills; and the use of the Internet and CD ROM technology.

Media Specialist, Holmes Elementary, Mesa School District, AZ (1993-1995). Teacher of library skills, on line computer research, literature appreciation; story-teller, audio visual coordinator, Young Authors Program coordinator, school yearbook sponsor, member of School Management Team.

Additional Librarian Experience: Museum of Northern Arizona Research Center, Flagstaff, AZ (summer, 1973). Librarian/research assistant, National Science Foundation fellow.

Government Documents Librarian, Cline Library, Northern Arizona University, Flagstaff, AZ (part-time 1972-74).

Management/
School
Administration

Director of Public Information, Durango School District, Colorado (1992-93). Directed community relations for 400 employees, 9 schools, 5,000 students. Responsible for public relations training of educational personnel, issues management, educational foundation liaison, media relations, writer/editor/photographer of all internal and external communications, coordinating finance referendum.

Information Officer, Paradise Valley School District, Phoenix, AZ (1985-1992). Directed community relations for 2,400 employees, 30 schools, and 27,000 students. Responsible for media relations, issues managment, communications and public relations training, founder of educational foundation, coordinator of internal staff incentive programs, grant and award writer, writer/editor/photographer of all internal and external communications, coordinated two finance referendums.

Communications Specialist, Flagstaff Public Schools, AZ (1983-85). Directed community relations for 900 employees, 14 schools, and 9,000 students. Responsible for media relations, communication and video training, writer/editor/photographer of all internal and external communications, coordinated district centennial community celebration, coordinated finance referendum.

Communications
Public Relations

Interim Director of Community Relations, Flagstaff Medical Center, AZ (Part-time, 1985). Directed public relations for major regional medical center. Coordinated finance referendum, coordinated open house activities, writer/editor/photographer of internal and external communications.

Communications and Community Relations Consultant for school districts in Arizona, Ohio, Kansas; corporations (Arizona Public Service, MacMillan Publishers); and organizations (City of Scottsdale, AZ, Prescott Public Library, Yavapai County Libraries, Prescott, AZ) in Colorado, Arizona, Ohio, and California. Presented seminars and workshops on group cooperation and leadership skills, crisis management, public speaking and sales skills, grant and award writing, newsletter and publications writing, video production and media relations.

Teaching Experience

Instructor of School Community Relations, Arizona State University, Tempe, AZ (Fall semesters, 1989-91).

Instructor of Public Relations, Rio Salado Community College, Phoenix, AZ (Spring semester, 1986).

Instructor of Communication, Northern Arizona University, Flagstaff, AZ (Fall semesters, 1976, 1983-85).

Instructor of Communication and Associate Director of Forensic Speech Activities, Miami University, Oxford, OH (1980-82). Taught Interpersonal Communication, Fundamentals of Public Speaking, Small Group Communication, Technical Communication, and coached the nationally ranked individual events speech team and the United States national oratorical champion.

Instructor of Mass Communication, Miami University, Oxford, OH (1979-80). Taught Television Production, Broadcast Journalism, Introduction to Mass Media Technology, Advanced Television Production, and Direction and Television Production Internship.

Instructor of Television Production, Yavapai Community College, Prescott, AZ (Fall semester, 1978).

Instructor of Speech, Drama and Television, Prescott High School, Prescott, AZ (1975-79). Taught Television Production, Oral Communication, Debate, Theatre, Television Internship and coordinated closed-circuit student-run television station that broadcast via cable to the community; coached state and nationally ranked speech and debate team.

Technology

Public Access Television Production Coordinator, United Cable Television of Scottsdale, AZ (1982-83). Coordinated video training for the City of Scottsdale, AZ, including city employees, non-profit organizations, public schools, Scottsdale Memorial Hospital and related health organizations; producer of local community programming.

Producer/Director of Videotaped Programming, Timothy Marcum Memorial Conference Center, Miami University, Oxford, OH (Summer, 1982). Produced videotapes to be used in conjunction with the professional conferences for world wide business and education conducted at the center.

PROFESSIONAL AFFILIATIONS AND PUBLICATIONS

Madison Educational Foundation, Madison School District, Phoenix, AZ (1998-2000). Chair of teacher minigrant program.

Teacher Venture Arizona Foundation for sponsorship of teacher minigrant, Vice President of Communications, Board of Directors, (1986-1998).

Arizona AWARE Women's Educational Administrators' State Association, president (1988-89); member (1985-91).

Alpha Delta Kappa, educational honorary sorority, president (1988-90); member (1984-1991).

National School Public Relations Association, member (1985-1993).

Arizona School Public Relations Association, president (1986-87); member, board of directors (1984-1992).

Phi Delta Kappa educational honorary, public relations director (1988-89); member (1987-1991).

American Cancer Society, Flagstaff, AZ, board of directors (1985-86).

Public Relations Professionals of Flagstaff, AZ, founder (1984-85).

PUBLICATIONS Published in several state and national publications (available upon request). Worked as a freelance writer for *It Starts on the Frontline,* published by the National School Public Relations Association in Rockville, Maryland.

SPECIAL RECOGNITION Teacher Venture Arizona Grant to sponsor a Multicultural Literature Celebration, and Hopi, Apache, and Tewa Native American professional children's author Michael LaCapa (fall, 1999).

City of Phoenix Block Watch grant to sponsor summer library programs for children (summers, 1998 and 1999, 2000).

Phoenix Arts Commission Artist in Residence Grant to construct a mosaic and acrylic mural depicting the theme *Let Citizenship Ring* at Camelview Elementary School (1999-2000).

Arizona School Public Relations Association Award of Excellence for a comprehensive school public relations program (1985, 1987, 1990, 1991).

National School Public Relations Association Golden Achievement Award for outstanding public relations campaigns (1986-88, 1990).

Arizona AWARE Women's Administrators' Association Golden Pen Award for outstanding written contributions to the field of education (1988).

Arizona School Administrators' Association Distinguished Administrator Award (1988).

National Community Education Association national photo award (1985).

Appendix H

Directory of State Humanities Councils, Spring 2000

Alabama Humanities Foundation
1100 Ireland Way, Suite 101
Birmingham, AL 35205-7001
Tel: 205/558-3980
Fax: 205/558-3981
Chair: Ann Boozer
Ex. Dir.: Robert Stewart
e-mail: rstewart@ahf.net

Alaska Humanities Forum
421 West First Avenue, Suite 210
Anchorage, AK 99501
Tel: 907/272-5341
Fax: 907/272-3979
Chair: Steve Haycox
Ex. Dir.: Steve Lindbeck
e-mail: forum@alaska.net

Amerika Samoa Humanities Council
P.O. Box 5800
Pago Pago, Amerikan Samoa 96799
Tel: 684/633-4870/4871
Fax: 684/633-4873
Chair: Lui Tuitele
Ex. Dir.: Niualama E. Taifane
e-mail: ashe@samoatelco.com

Arizona Humanities Council
Ellis-Shackelford House
1242 North Central Avenue
Phoenix, AZ 85004
Tel: 602/257-0335
Fax: 602/257-0392
Chair: Joel Hiller
Ex. Dir.: Dan Shilling
e-mail: dan.shilling@asu.edu

Arkansas Humanities Council
10816 Executive Center Drive
Suite 310
Little Rock, AR 72211
Tel: 501/221-0091
Fax: 501/221-9860
Chair: Paul Austin
Ex. Dir: Robert Bailey

California Council for the Humanities
312 Sutter, Suite 601
San Francisco, CA 94108
Tel: 415/391-1474
Fax: 415/391-1312
Chair: Isabel Alegria
        David Mas Masumoto
Ex. Dir.: James Quay
e-mail: cch@calhum.org

Felicia Kelley
Program Officer
315 West 9th Street, Suite 702
Los Angeles, CA 90015
Tel: 213/623-5993
Fax: 213/623-6833
e-mail: fkelly@calhum.org

Amy Rouillard
Program Officer
614 Fifth Street
Suite C
San Diego, CA 92101
Tel: 619/232-4020
Fax: 619/232-4025
e-mail: amyr@calhum.org

Colorado Endowment for the Humanities

1490 Lafayette St., Suite 101
Denver, CO 80218
Tel: 303/894-7951
Fax: 303/864-9361
Chair: Camila A. Alire
Ex. Dir: Margaret A. Coval
e-mail: ceh@ceh.org

Commonwealth of the Northern Mariana Islands Council for the Humanities

AAA-3394 Box 10001
Saipan, MP 96950
Tel: 670/235-4785
Fax: 670/235-4786
Chair: Herman T. Guerrero
Ex. Dir.: William R. Barrineau
e-mail: humanities@saipan.com

Connecticut Humanities Council

955 South Main Street, Suite E
Middletown, CT 06457
Tel: 860/685-2260
Fax: 860/704-0429
Chair: Helen Higgins
Ex. Dir.: Bruce Fraser
e-mail: lcomstock@wesleyan.edu

Delaware Humanities Forum

Community Services Building
100 West Tenth Street, Suite 1009
Wilmington, DE 19801
Tel: 302/657-0650
Fax: 302/657-0655
Toll: 800/752-2060
Chair: Susan T. Shoemaker
Acting Ex. Dir.: Joseph E. Johnson
e-mail: hhofmann@dca.net

Humanities Council of Washington, D.C.

1331 H Street, NW, Suite 902
Washington, DC 20005
Tel: 202/347-1732
Fax: 202/347-3350
Chair: Alice L. Norris
Ex. Dir.: Linn Shapiro
e-mail: hcwdc@humanities-wdc.org

Florida Humanities Council

1725 1/2 East Seventh Avenue
Tampa, FL 33605
Tel: 813/272-3473
Fax: 813/272-3314
Chair: Lloyd Chapin
Ex. Dir.: Fran Cary
e-mail: fhc@flahum.org

Georgia Humanities Council

50 Hurt Plaza, SE
Suite 1565
Atlanta, GA 30303-2915
Tel: 404/523-6220
Fax: 404/523-5702
Toll: 800/523-6202
Chair: Emma Adler
President: Jamil S. Zainaldin
e-mail: ghc@emory.edu

Guam Humanities Council

Suite 101 Center Pointe Bldg.
426 Chalan San Antonio
Tamuning, Guam 96911
Tel: 671/646-4461
Fax: 671/646-2243
Chair: Marilyn Sagas
Ex. Dir.: Jillette Leon-Guerrero
e-mail: ghc@kuentos.guam.net

Hawaii Council for the Humanities

3599 Wai'alae Avenue, Room 23
Honolulu, HI 96816
Tel: 808/732-5402
Fax: 808/732-5402
Chair: Mitch Yamasaki
Ex. Dir.: Annette Lew
e-mail: hch@aloha.net

Idaho Humanities Council
217 West State Street
Boise, ID 83702
Tel: 208/345-5346
Fax: 208/345-5347
Chair: Kurt Olsson
Ex. Dir.: Rick Ardinger
e-mail: rickihc@micron.net

Illinois Humanities Council
203 North Wabash
Suite 2020
Chicago, IL 60601
Tel: 312/422-5580
Fax: 312/422-5588
Chair: Jack Wing
Ex. Dir.: Kristina Valaitis
e-mail: ihc@prairie.org

Indiana Humanities Council
1500 North Delaware Street
Indianapolis, IN 46202
Tel: 317/638-1500
Fax: 317/634-9503
Chair: Thomas Wilhelmus
Ex. Dir.: Scott Massey
e-mail: ihc@iupui.edu

Humanities Iowa
Northlawn, Oakdale Campus
Iowa City, IA 52242-5000
Tel: 319/335-4153
Fax: 319/335-4154
Chair: Fred Waldstein
Ex. Dir.: Christopher Rossi
e-mail: info@humanitiesiowa.org

Kansas Humanities Council
112 SW Sixth Avenue
Suite 210
Topeka, KS 66603-3895
Tel: 785/357-0359
Fax: 785/357-1723
Chair: Gayle Davis
Ex. Dir.: Marion Cott
e-mail: kshumcoun@aol.com

Kentucky Humanities Council
206 E. Maxwell
Lexington, KY 40508-2613
Tel: 606/257-5932
Fax: 606/257-5933
Chair: Roger J. Wolford
Ex. Dir.: Virginia Smith
e-mail: vgsmit00@pop.uky.edu

**Louisiana Endowment for
the Humanities**
225 Baronne Street
Suite 1414
New Orleans, LA 70112-1789
Tel: 504/523-4352
Fax: 504/529-2358
Toll: 800/909-7990
Chair: Rosemary Ewing
President: Michael Sartisky
e-mail: leh@leh.org

Maine Humanities Council
371 Cumberland Avenue
P.O. Box 7202
Portland, ME 04112
Tel: 207/773-5051
Fax: 207/773-2416
Co-Chairs: Geoffrey Gratwick
Ex. Dir.: Dorothy Schwartz
e-mail: info@mainehumanities.org

Maryland Humanities Council
Executive Plaza One, Suite 503
11350 McCormick Road
Hunt Valley, MD 21031-1002
Tel: 410/771-0650
Fax: 410/771-0655
Chair: Rhoda Dorsey
Ex. Dir.: Barbara Wells Sarudy
e-mail: pWeber@mdhc.org

Massachusetts Foundation for the Humanities

One Woodbridge Street
South Hadley, MA 01075
Tel: 413/536-1385
Fax: 413/534-6918
Chair: David L. Smith
Ex. Dir.: David Tebaldi
e-mail: tebaldi@mfh.org

125 Walnut Street
Watertown, MA 02472
Tel: 617/923-1678
Fax: 617/426-5441
Associate Dir.: Ellen K. Rothman
e-mail: ekrothman@mfh.org

Michigan Humanities Council

119 Pere Marquette Drive, Suite 3B
Lansing, MI 48912-1270
Tel: 517/372-7770
Fax: 517/372-0027
Chair: Sheila Cannatti
Ex. Dir.: Rick Knupfer
e-mail: mihum@voyager.net

E4624 Highway M-35
Escanaba, MI 49829
Tel: 906/789-9471
Fax: 906/789-2568
Pub. Aff's. Ofc.: Nancy L. Mathews
e-mail: paomihum@voyager.net

Minnesota Humanities Commission

987 East Ivy Avenue
St. Paul, MN 55106-2046
Tel: 651/774-0105
Fax: 651/774-0205
Chair: W. Andrew Boss
President: Cheryl Dickson
e-mail: cheryld@thinkmhc.org

Mississippi Humanities Council

3825 Ridgewood Road, Room 311
Jackson, MS 39211-6453
Tel: 601/982-6752
Fax: 601/982-6750
Chair: Gemma Beckley
Ex. Dir.: Barbara Carpenter
e-mail: barbara@mhc.state.ms.us

Missouri Humanities Council

543 Hanley Industrial Court, Suite 201
St. Louis, MO 63144-1905
Tel: 314/781-9660
Fax: 314/781-9681
Chair: Randy Maness
Ex. Dir.: Michael Bouman
e-mail: mail@mohumanities.org

Montana Committee for the Humanities

311 Brantly Hall
The University of Montana
Missoula, MT 59812
Tel: 406/243-6022
Fax: 406/243-4836
Toll: 800/624-6001
Chair: Frederick Skinner
Ex. Dir.: Mark Sherouse
e-mail: lastbest@selway.umt.edu

Nebraska Humanities Council

Lincoln Ctr. Bldg., #225
215 Centennial Mall South
Lincoln, NE 68508
Tel: 402/474-2131
Fax: 402/474-4852
Chair: Pam Snow
Ex. Dir.: Jane Hood
e-mail: nehumanities@juno.com

Nevada Humanities Committee
P.O. Box 8029
Reno, NV 89507
Tel: 775/784-6587
Fax: 775/784-6527
Toll: 800/382-5023 (Las Vegas office)
Chair: Christopher Hudgins
Ex. Dir.: Judith Winzeler
e-mail: winzeler@scs.unr.edu

Nevada Humanities Committee
(Las Vegas office)
4505 Maryland Parkway, FDH 551
Box 455080
Las Vegas, NV 89154-5080
Tel: 702/895-1878
Fax: 702/895-1877
Program Coordinator: David Mishler
e-mail: dmishler@nevada.edu

New Hampshire Humanities Council
19 Pillsbury Street
P.O. Box 2228
Concord, NH 03302-2228
Tel: 603/224-4071
Fax: 603/224-4072
Chair: Joseph Marcille
Ex. Dir.: Charles Bickford
e-mail: nhhum@nhhc.org

New Jersey Council for the Humanities
28 West State Street, Sixth Floor
Trenton, NJ 08608
Tel: 609/695-4838
Fax: 609/695-4929
Chair: Barry V. Qualls
Ex. Dir.: Jane Rutkoff
e-mail: njch@njch.org

New Mexico Endowment for the Humanities
209 Onate Hall
Corner of Campus & Girard NE
Albuquerque, NM 87131
Tel: 505/277-3705
Fax: 505/277-6056
Chair: Linda Aycock
Ex. Dir.: Craig Newbill
e-mail: nmeh@unm.edu

New York Council for the Humanities
150 Broadway, Suite 1700
New York, NY 10038
Tel: 212/233-1131
Fax: 212/233-4607
Chair: Samuel Waksal
Ex. Dir.: Jay Kaplan
e-mail: hum@echonyc.com

North Carolina Humanities Council
200 South Elm Street, Suite 403
Greensboro, NC 27401
Tel: 336/334-5325
Fax: 336/334-5052
Chair: Elizabeth Minnich
Ex. Dir.: Alice Barkley
e-mail: NCHC@gborocollege.edu

North Dakota Humanities Council
P.O. Box 2191
Bismarck, ND 58502
Tel: 701/255-3360
Fax: 701/223-8724
Toll: 800/338-6543
Chair: Carol Cashman
Ex. Dir.: Everett Albers
e-mail: ealbers@nd-humanities.org

Ohio Humanities Council
695 Bryden Road
P.O. Box 06354
Columbus, OH 43206-0354
Tel: 614/461-7802
Fax: 614/461-4651
Chair: George Garrison
Ex. Dir.: Gale Peterson
e-mail: ohiohum@aol.com

Oklahoma Humanities Council

428 West California, Suite 270
Oklahoma City, OK 73102
Tel: 405/235-0280
Fax: 405/235-0289
Chair: David Levy
Ex. Dir.: Anita May
e-mail: okhum@flash.net

Oregon Council for the Humanities

812 SW Washington, Suite 225
Portland, OR 97205
Tel: 503/241-0543
Fax: 503/241-0024
Toll: 800/735-0543
Chair: Brad Reddersen
Ex. Dir.: Christopher Zinn
e-mail: och@oregonhum.org

Pennsylvania Humanities Council

325 Chestnut Street, #715
Philadelphia, PA 19106-2607
Tel: 215/925-1005
Fax: 215/925-3054
Chair: C. James Trotman
Ex. Dir.: Joseph J. Kelly
e-mail: phc@libertynet.org

Fundacion Puertorriquena de las Humanidades

P.O. Box 9023920
San Juan de Puerto Rico 00902-3920
Tel: 787/721-2087
Fax: 787/721-2684
Chair: Ana H. Quintero
Ex. Dir.: Juan M. Gonzalez Lamela

Rhode Island Committee for the Humanities

60 Ship Street
Providence, RI 02903
Tel: 401/273-2250
Fax: 401/454-4872
Chair: Galen A. Johnson
Ex. Dir.: M. Drake Patten
e-mail: ri_ch@ids.net

South Carolina Humanities Council

P.O. Box 5287
Columbia, SC 29250
Tel: 803/691-4100
Fax: 803/691-0809
Chair: S.C. "Cal" McMeekin, Jr.
Ex. Dir.: Randy Akers
e-mail: bobschc@aol.com

South Dakota Humanities Council

Box 7050, University Station
Brookings, SD 57007
Tel: 605/688-6113
Fax: 605/688-4531
Chair: Sid Goss
Ex. Dir.: Michael Haug
e-mail: sdhc@ur.sdstate.edu

Tennessee Humanities Council

1003 18th Avenue South
Nashville, TN 37212
Tel: 615/320-7001
Fax: 615/321-4586
Chair: Linda Caldwell
Ex. Dir.: Robert Cheatham
e-mail: robert@tn-humanities.org

Texas Council for the Humanities

Banister Place A
3809 S. Second Street
Austin, TX 78704
Tel: 512/440-1991
Fax: 512/440-0115
Chair: Wright L. Lassiter, Jr.
Ex. Dir.: Monte Youngs
e-mail: postmaster
@public-humanities.org

Utah Humanities Council

202 West 300 North
Salt Lake City, UT 84103-1108
Tel: 801/359-9670
Fax: 801/531-7869
Chair: France Davis
Ex. Dir.: Cynthia Buckingham
e-mail:
buckingham@utahhumanities.org

Vermont Council on the Humanities
200 Park Street
Morrisville, VT 05661
Tel: 802/888-3183
Fax: 802/888-1236
Chair: Charles R. Putney
Ex. Dir.: Victor Swenson
e-mail: vch@together.net

Virgin Islands Humanities Council
5-6 Kongens Gade
Corbiere Complex, Suites 200B & 201B
St. Thomas, USVI 00802
Tel: 340/776-4044
Fax: 340/774-3972
Chair: Roach A. Tregenza
Ex. Dir.: Magda Smith
e-mail: vihc@viaccess.net

Virginia Foundation for the Humanities
145 Ednam Drive
Charlottesville, VA 22903
Tel: 804/924-3296
Fax: 804/296-4714
Chair: Wyndham B. Blanton, Jr.
President: Robert Vaughan
e-mail: rcv@virginia.edu

**Washington Commission for
the Humanities**
615 Second Avenue, Suite 300
Seattle, WA 98104
Tel: 206/682-1770
Fax: 206/682-4158
Chair: Grace Millay Ott
Ex. Dir.: Margaret Ann Bollmeier
e-mail: wch@humanities.org

West Virginia Humanities Council
723 Kanawha Blvd. East, Suite 800
Charleston, WV 25301
Tel: 304/346-8500
Fax: 304/346-8504
Chair: Joseph Jefferds
Ex. Dir.: Ken Sullivan
e-mail: wvhuman@wvhc.com

Wisconsin Humanities Council
222 S. Bedford St., Suite F
Madison, WI 53703-3688
Tel: 608/262-0706
Fax: 608/263-7970
Chair: Mary Gielow
Ex. Dir.: Max R. Harris
e-mail: whc@danenet.org

Wyoming Council for the Humanities
P.O. Box 3643
Laramie, WY 82071-3643
Tel: 307/766-6496
Fax: 307/742-4914
Chair: Lokey Lytjen
Ex. Dir.: Robert G. Young
e-mail: hummer@uwyo.edu

Appendix I

Technology Inventory

Date _____   Librarian _____   School _____

Location	Type of Hardware	Manufacturer	Model	Serial Number	Asset Tag	Comments
(Example: Library or Computer Lab)	(Example: CPU, Monitor, Printer)	(Example: IBM, MAC, Compaq)			(Bar code	
Example:						
Library	CPU	Compaq	1234567	88999	X	

Appendix J

Application

Do not include the name of your school (or anything that would identify your school) in your application.

Project Title: _____
Number of students who will participate: _____
Amount requested: _____
Applicant's Position: _____
Grade/Department: _____
Please provide the following information:

1. Purpose of request
2. Implementation plan
3. Timetable (Funds must be used during second semester 2002.)
4. Outcomes: How will you determine the success of your program? What outcomes are you seeking?
5. Evaluation: Explain your evaluation tool and how it will be used.
6. How is this project innovative?
7. How is the program in alignment with the curriculum?
8. Does this program support your school improvement plan? How?
9. Does the proposed program have a community involvement component? ____ Yes ____ No If yes, describe.
10. If you receive funding for this project, can you sustain it for future years? If so, please describe your plan to cover future expenses, provide necessary staffing, and continue community involvement, if applicable.
11. Please provide a detailed budget. Are there items in your budget that could be covered in your school budget? ____ Yes ____ No If yes, which items?

Items	Expense	Funding Source

12. Are you seeking funds from other sources in addition to SMEF? ____ Yes ____ No If yes, from whom?

What Happens After The Deadline?

All applicants will be notified about the status of their grant after December 12. Awardees will be able to access their grant funds after this date.

Grant recipients are required to submit a final report by May 31, 2002. The final report must include an accounting of how funds were spent, how project will be implemented in subsequent years, and an evaluation of outcomes. A report form will be provided to all awardees.

Shawnee Mission
Education Foundation

7235 Antioch
Shawnee Mission, KS 66204
(913) 993-9360   FAX (913) 993-9364
Visit us at www.smef.org

The Shawnee Mission Education Foundation will provide private funding of innovative programs and creative teaching methods to enhance the learning opportunities for every Shawnee Mission School District student.

E² Grant Program

Excellence in Education

ATTN: SMSD Educators

Subject: **E² Grant Program**

The Shawnee Mission Education Foundation is now accepting grant applications for the Excellence in Education (E²) grant program.

K-12 educators are eligible to apply for funds of up to $5,000 for creative projects.

Be sure to get your application in before the November 2 deadline!

Shawnee Mission
Education Foundation

What is E²?

E² grants are designed to provide varying levels of funding of up to $5,000 for creative projects implemented by schools, school departments, teachers, librarians, counselors, nurses, and other district educators. Grants will be awarded to educators who develop projects that the district is unable to fund. K-12 educators may apply.

Educators who received E² grants for the 2000-2001 school year are ineligible to apply for 2001-2002 E² grants.

To Apply for an E² Grant:

- Application (not counting cover page) should be no longer than 4 pages. If submitting application via e-mail, cover page should be on a page by itself.
- Submit application as follows:
  - a. Hard copy: 9 copies—no faxes

  OR
  - b. E-mail: submit your application as a Word document attachment to adjohnst@smsd.org.
- Use no smaller than an 11-point font and 1" margins.
- To see a sample grant application that has been funded, please contact the SMEF office at (913) 993-9360 or e-mail adjohnst@smsd.org.

Application Deadline

Friday November 2, 2001 by 5:00 p.m. Applications received after this time will be excluded.

E² is the only Foundation grant program being offered in 2001-2002. **Take advantage of this opportunity and apply now!**

What is the Criteria for Funding?

The Foundation will fund projects that:

- Are innovative.
- Enhance the school/department/classroom/ educator curriculum. Grants are not limited to individual teachers or schools. Innovative projects that involve collaboration within a department or a collaborative effort involving multiple teachers or schools will be considered favorably.
- Can be sustained beyond the initial year of funding.
- Provide an evaluation component.
- Involve the local community (Although this element is not required, the Foundation will look favorably at applications that involve the community.)
- Include a detailed budget.
- Are available to a broad spectrum of students. Grants of varying sizes will be awarded. The size of the grant will be evaluated in relation to the number of students impacted by the grant.
- Will be implemented during the spring 2002 semester.

The Foundation will not Fund:

- Programs, projects, materials that can be included in the school budget.
- Building improvements that do not have an educational component, i.e., benches, paving, cabinets, paint, etc.
- Honoraria, teacher salaries or substitute educator expenses.

Approval of this proposed project is solely for the purpose of awarding a grant. The Shawnee Mission Education Foundation Board of Directors does not make any judgment on or approve the particular details, procedures, or activities of the proposed project and shall in no way be liable for injuries or damages arising from the proposed project.

Cover Page—Include with Application—Please Print Neatly!

School_____ Phone_____ Email_____

Department_____ Classroom_____

Project Title (*Do not include name of school in project title.*)_____

Number of students who will participate in project_____ Student Population_____

Applicant's Name and Position_____

Principal's Signature_____ Date_____

If application is submitted by email, principal must email his/her approval of grant application by Friday, November 2 at 5:00 p.m.

Appendix K

Listservs for School Librarians

AASLFORUM is offered to all personal members of AASL Members Forum. They may also subscribe to the specialized discussion list exclusively for their subsection: Educators of Library Media Specialists Section (ELMSS), Independent Schools Section (ISS), or Supervisors Section (SPVS).

To subscribe to any of these lists, send an e-mail message to *listproc@ala.org*. In the subject line of the message, type **subscribe**. For the first and only line of text in the body of the message type **subscribe list-name Your name member #**.

Substitute the name of the list to which you wish to subscribe, i.e., AASLFORUM, ELMSS, ISS or SPVS, and your first and last names. Your request must include your ALA personal member number.

LM_NET is an international listserv for school library media specialists on the Internet. To join, send an e-mail message to *listserv@listserv.syr.edu*. Place nothing in the subject line, and the words **subscribe lm_net** and your name in the body of the message.

IASL-LINK, the listserv of the International Association of School Librarianship (IASL), offers international networking. To join, send an e-mail message to *anne@rhi.hi.is* with your name and country.

ATLC FORUM, the listserv of the Association for Teacher Librarianship in Canada, welcomes members from outside Canada. To join, send an e-mail to *listproc@camosun.bc.ca*. Put nothing in the subject line, and the words **subscribe atlcforum** with your name in the body of the message.

AASL News, the listserv of the American Association of School Librarians (AASL), is a "read only" listserv open to AASL members and nonmembers. To subscribe, send an e-mail message to *listproc@ala.org*. Put nothing in the subject line and the words **subscribe aaslnews** in the body of the message. Add your first name, followed by your last name.

Bring Home the Bacon is an electronic newsletter sponsored by *SchoolGrants*. To join, send a message to *Listserv@netpals.lsoft.com*. In the body of the message, type the following commands: **SUBSCRIBE BRINGHOMEBACON YourFirstName YourLastName**.To subscribe to their monthly newsletter, send a blank e-mail requesting **subscribe@schoolgrants.org**.

BIG6 is a worldwide discussion group for school library media specialists and other educators interested in the Big 6 Skills approach to information literacy skills instruction. To join, send an e-mail to *LITSERV@listserv.syr.edu* with nothing in the subject line. Add the words subscribe Big6 and your name in the body of the message.

BooKBrag, sponsored by the Scholastic Network for teachers and librarians, contains a monthly newsletter, book reviews, author talk, and input from teachers. To subscribe, send an e-mail to *BooKBrag-request@scholastic.com*. Put nothing in the subject line. In the body of the message type the words **subscribe bookbrag** and your name.

CCBC-NET is set by the School of Education, University of Wisconsin-Madison, to encourage the discussion of books for children and young adults. To join, send an e-mail message to *listserv@ccbc.soemadison.wisc.edu* with the following in the subject line: **sub ccbc-net yourfirstname yourlast name**.

EDInfo will keep you updated on government grant opportunities. To subscribe, address an e-mail message to *listproc@inet.ed.gov*. Then write **SUBSCRIBE EDINFO YOURFIRSTNAME YOURLASTNAME** in the message.

EDTECH is a listserv for the discussion of all aspects of technology and its use in education. To join, send an e-mail to *listserv@smsu.edu*. Put nothing in the subject line. Within the body of the message place the words **subscribe edtech** and your name.

KIDLIT-L is for you if you are interested in discussing children's literature online. To join, send an e-mail to *listserv@bingvmb.cc.binghampton.edu*, placing nothing in the subject line. In the body of the message, put the words **subscribe kidlit-l** and your name.

PND-L. Philanthropy News Digest will send you an e-mail version of *Philanthropy News Digest*, the Foundation Center's digest of philanthropy-related news once a week if you sign up. Send a message to *LISTSERV@LIST>FDNCENTER.ORG* with the words SUBSCRIBE PND-L and your name in the message.

Appendix L

Sample Budget American Grant Act**

Project Title: Research Online
Project Applicant: Washington School District

Local Reform Application - FY02
November 1, 2002 – June 30, 2003

ALL FUNDS SHOULD BE EXPENDED BY JUNE 30, 2003. An individual local education agency or a consortium applicant may apply for a minimum of $6,000 or a maximum amount not to exceed $3 per student.

Account Name	Direct Cost Categories Description	Moneys Requested From Grant	Local Effort	Other Sources
(The items listed under each category are not all inclusive and the applicant is not required to request funds in each category.)	Project Coordinator		16,000	
Personnel Salary/wages (Substitute pay, stipends, and so on would be addressed under this line item)	Teacher stipends for 45 librarians and facilitators for approx. 52 hours of training	36,122		
	Extra duty stipend for secretaries for data entry	2,000		
Personnel Benefits	FICA for stipends	3,060		
Travel	Travel for project coordinator to state and national meetings	2,000		
*Equipment (list) (Equipment request will be reviewed very closely)	Internet file server	4,000	6,000	
Supplies and Materials (Office and educational)	Assessment materials and books, Web editors, binders, forms, and other miscellaneous supplies	2,000 1,500		
Evaluation of Project (Data collections and analysis, consultants, reports)	Development and dissemination of evaluation materials	1,500		
Contractual (Consultants, subcontracts, mini-grants)	Web site design consultant	30,000		
	Performance assessment consultant	2,000	4,000	
	Web site maintenance contact	8,000		
	Travel for consultant	2,000		
General Operating Costs (Duplicating, postage, room rental, telephone)	Duplication	500		
	Phones	50		
	Postage	50		
General Administration (May not exceed 5% of budget. Includes activities concerned with establishing and administering policy for operating the district.)				

*These line items may not exceed 10% of total budget

	Totals	94,782	26,000	

Budget Narrative

This application includes activities and strategies to develop and implement a local improvement plan that meets the requirements of the American Grant Act and will not result in a significant increase in paperwork for teachers.

At least 95 percent of the subgrant funds received will go directly to improve the curriculum and instruction in the schools in our district. More than 50 percent of the funds will go to schools with a special need for assistance. The fourteen schools selected for participation include all the Title I schools in the district. At the middle school level, the two lowest-achieving schools (out of seven) were chosen. The lowest-scoring of the five high schools was also included. The selected schools contain the district's highest concentration of students receiving free and reduced-cost lunches.

About the Author

Cynthia Anderson is the director of library and media services for a large suburban school district. During her 25 years in education, she has been a school librarian and an elementary school principal. Cynthia won the Milken Family Foundation Educator Award in 1994 and was honored when *Redbook Magazine* selected her elementary school as one of the best schools in America in 1995.

Her articles have been published in *Knowledge Quest, Library Talk, Reading Teacher, School Library Media Activities Monthly, and The School Librarian's Worksho*p.

Cynthia lives in Fairway, Kansas, with her Pug dog, Emma, and stacks of good books, read and unread.

Index

A

Abstract, 34, 41, 69
Academic achievement, 44
  fraternities, 20
Accounting system, 88
Acronyms, 56, 63
American Association of School
  Librarians (AASL), 20, 24, 85
American Libraries, 17, 24
American Library Association
  (ALA), 14-15, 20
  ALA's New Member Round
  Table (NMRT), 14
  scholarship committee, 24
American Society For Curriculum
  Development (ASCD), 20
American With Disabilities Act (ADA), 6
Anecdotal information, 49
Annual reports, 16-17, 20-22
Appearance, 60
Appendix(es), 53, 62, 71, 72
Application, 18, 33, 74
  forms, 17
  processes, 12
Applying, 79
Articles, 52, 71, 82, 84
Assembly, 72
Assessment, 49
  authentic, 44, 55
  performance-based, 49
  student-centered, 67
Associations, 18, 20, 84
Attachments, 30, 34, 53
Attendance records, 51
Auditor, 89
Author visit, 8
Award descriptions, 53

B

Benchmarks, 43
Big picture, 2
Biographical sketches, 48
Biographies, 71
Blue Ribbon of Excellence Award, 85
Bookkeeping, 88
Bookmarks, 13, 83
Book Report, 17
Boolean search tips, 15
Boston, 20
Boston Center for Adult Education, 20
Brain-based education, 55
Brainstorm, 3, 8, 31
Brochures, 52, 53, 84, 131
Budget, 9, 29, 40, 45, 59, 71, 74, 76, 88
  business office, 70
  categories, 45
  dissemination activities, 51
  estimate, 46
  expenditures, 50, 88
  in-kind, 45
  narrative, 29, 44
  phases, 45
  other costs, 46
  restrictions, 34
  salaries, 46
  sample, 135
Bullets, 60-61
Buros, 50
Business manager, 32
Business office, 30, 70, 72, 88
Buzzwords, 34

C

Cable in the Classroom, 17
Capital funds, 2
*Catalog of Federal Domestic
  Assistance*, 16
Cautions, 6, 47
Center for Nonprofit Management, 20

Certification, 52
Chamber of Commerce, 13
Chart, 60
Checklist, 70
Cicero, 3
Circulation desk, 6-7
Clarity, 55
Clichés, 57, 63
Clippings, 71, 84, 89
Confidentiality, 26
Collaborate, 21, 31
Collaboration, 74
Collection development, 6
Communications, 45
Community foundations, 14
Company-sponsored foundations, 14
Concept paper, 38
Conferences, 5, 20, 52, 85
Consultant(s), 29, 45, 46
Consultation, 51
Contacts, 12
Content, 66
Contest(s), 9, 24
Contracts, 45
Cooperative learning, 29
Copies, 30, 32, 34-35, 70-72
Copy maker, 30
Corporate 500 Directory of Corporate Philanthropy, 16
Corporate Giving Directory, 16
Corporate Foundations, 14
Corporations, 12-14
Cost sharing, 45
Council on Foundations, 16
Cover letter, 26, 39-40, 71-72
Credentials, 4, 41, 48
Credibility, 68
Cultural diversity, 6
Curriculum vita, 4, 24, 25, 48, 82
Curriculum-based measurement, 55

D

Data, 29, 42, 51, 89
    demographic, 42
Date due, 35, 89
    interim, 35, 54
Daughters of the American Revolution (DAR), 13, 18
de Cervantes, Miguel, 73
de la Bruyere, Jean, 65
Deadline(s), 35, 62, 69-70
    internal, 31
Delivery person, 30
Demonstrations, 52
Department of Education (ED), 26
Dialog, 19
Directories, 16-17
    Corporate 500: The Directory of Corporate Philanthropy, 16
    Corporate Giving Directory, 16
    Foundation Directory, 16
    Foundation Directory, Part 2, 16
    Foundation Grants to Individuals, 17
    National Directory of Corporate Giving of Foundations, 21
    Statistical Abstract of the United States Directory of State Humanities Councils, 15, 123
Disk, 36
Disney Learning Partnership Grant, 67
Dissemination, 51-52, 83
Diversity, 6
Documentation, 76, 88
Dream Team, 2
Dream(s), 1, 2, 9

E

E-books, 6
E-Rate, 5
e-school News, 17
Editing, 72, 78
Editor, 30, 69, 74
Education Department (ED) grants, 15
Education foundations, 25

Educational Testing Service (ETS), 50
Educator's Guide to Evaluating the Use of Technology in Schools and Classrooms, 50
Electronic discussion group, 19
Electronic school, 17
Employee benefits, 45
Endorsements, 71
English Language Learners (ELL), 56
Enrollment records, 51
Environment, 7
Equipment, 5, 45, 90
   specifications, 71
ERIC search, 29, 42
Errors in grant writing, 28, 76
ETS Collection Catalog, 50
Evaluation, 43, 49, 76, 87, 89-90
   consultation, 51
   formative, 49
   interim reports, 51
   methods, 50
   summative, 49
   technology, 49
   test resources, 50
Examples, 57
Executive summary, 41
Experience, 77
Extensions, 90
Ezra Jack Keats Foundation, 14

F

Facility needs, 7
Family literacy, 44
Federal/government grants, 14-15, 26
Federal Register, 16
Feedback, 77
Feng shui, 7
FICA deductions, 29, 45
Field reader, 26
Filler, 63
Financial statements, 71
First draft, 65
Fluff, 57, 63
Follett, 24

Follow directions, 69, 75
Font, 29, 33, 62
Format, 31, 58, 63
Formative evaluation, 49
Formatting rules, 33
Foundation Center, 16, 20-21
Foundation Directory, 16
Foundation Directory, Part 2, 16
Foundation Grants to Individuals, 17
Foundations, types of, 13
   community, 14
   company-sponsored, 14
   independent or private, 13
From Now On: The Educational Technology Journal, 19
Funding sources, 12,
Furniture, 7

G

Gandhi, Mahatma, 87
Generic, 47
Goals and objectives, 10, 43
Goals 2000, 43
Government funds, 14
Grant Award Actions Database, 15
Grant reader, 23-28
   responsibilities, 27
Grant writing team, 28, 74
   abstract writer, 29
   copy maker, 30
   delivery person, 30
   editor, 30
   key communicator, 30
   number cruncher, 29
   pace keeper, 31
   proofreader, 30
   reader, 29
   researcher, 29
   shopper, 29
   statistician, 29
   veteran, 30
GRANTS Database, 19
Grantswriters.com, 19
Graph(s), 42, 60

Graphic organizer, 60-61
Graphics, 60
*Grants & Funding For School
Technology,* 20
Grolier, 24
Group norms, 31
Guidelines, 16, 17, 62, 70, 72, 75, 76, 89

H

Handicap accessibility, 6
Handwriting, 70
Headings, 30, 61, 66
Higher Education Field Reader
System, 26
Highlight(ing), 21, 29, 31, 33, 34, 53,
59, 63
Honorarium, 26
Horn Book, 17
*Humanities Projects in Libraries
and Archives,* 15

I

IBM, 21
Independent foundations, 13
Individualized Educational
Program (IEP), 56
Informal reading inventory, 49
In-kind, 45
Inquiry, 4
Integrated learning, 67
Internal review team, 28
International Reading
Association (IRA), 24, 86
Internet searches, 15, 22
Iowa Test of Basic Skills (ITBS), 43
IRS Form 501(c)3, 53

J

Jargon, 56, 58, 62
Job descriptions, 48
Johnson, Samuel, 55
Journal articles, 5, 42, 52, 53, 82, 84
Journals, 2-4, 10, 17, 19, 84
Judge contests, 24, 32

K

Key communicator, 30
Kirshstein, Rita, 50
Knowledge Express Data Systems, 19
Knowledge Quest, 17

L

*Learning and Leading with
Technology,* 17
Legal counsel, 18
Leonardo da Vinci, 8
Lesley College, 20
Letter
cover, 26, 39, 71-72
notification, 82
of appreciation, 81
of inquiry, 4
of intent, 15
proposal, 38
support, 52, 69
Library coordinator, 30
Library Journal, 17
Library Services and
Construction Act (LSCA), 15
handbook, 15
Library Services and
Technology Act (LSTA), 15
Library Talk, 17
Library technology, 5
Lion's Club, 86
List(s), 61, 63, 66
Listservs, 19, 22, 29, 133
Local community, 83, 86
Local foundations, 25
Long-range plans, 2, 5, 8
Lounge furniture, 7

M

Mailing, 72
address, 34
Margins, 61
Matching funds, 47
Materials and supplies, 46

Mechanics, 66
Media and Methods, 17
Media storage, 7
Meeting schedules, 31
Memorials, 8
Mentoring programs, 7
Miller, Olin, 39
Mission or mission statement, 4, 9, 11, 41, 43, 76
Multicultural events, 7
  materials, 6
Multiple funding sources, 47, 79
Multiple submissions, 38

N

NASA, 57
National Data Book, 17
National Directory of Corporate Giving, 17
National Education Association (NEA), 20, 86
National Endowment for the Humanities (NEH), 15
Needs assessment, 42
  statement, 18
net connect, 17
Network, 18, 78
New Member Round Table (NMRT), 14
News conferences, 83
Newsletter(s), 17, 83, 89
Newspaper articles, 42, 53, 71
Nichols, Dr. Beverly, ix, 67

O

Objectives, 10, 43, 51
  measurable, 43
Office of Postsecondary Education, 26
Organizational charts, 53
Outline, 31
Oversight committee, 89

P

Pace keeper, 31
Page numbers, 41
Pagination, 62
Partnerships, 31
Parts of proposal, 39
Patterns of giving, 12
Peers, 84
Personnel, 40, 41, 45, 47, 52
Phases, 45
Photos, 71
Pictures, 82, 84
Plan of action, 43
Planning meeting, 31
Plutarch, 11
Points, 34, 39
Portfolios, 48
Posters, 83
PowerPoint, 85
Presentation(s), 52, 85, 89
Presenting, 85
Press conferences, 52, 84
Press release, 82-84
Principal, 2-3, 6, 10, 28, 30, 32, 49, 70, 71, 83
Print media, 19
Print size, 33
Priorities, 34
Prioritize, 5
Private foundations, 13
Problem-based learning, 4, 44
Process (grant writing), 32
Professional associations, 20
Professional organizations, 20, 24
Program manager, 88-89
Program officer, 36, 38
Project
  Description, 44
  fact sheet, 84
  manager, 78
  newsletter, 51
  objectives, 10
  summary, 41

Proofreader, 30, 69, 74
Proofreading, 68, 70, 72
Proposal letter, 38
PTA, 8, 13, 83, 86
Publication Manual of the American Psychological Association, 68
Publicity, 45
Punch, 66, 72

Q

Query letter, 18, 22
Quinones, Sherri, 50

R

Rainbow Coalition, 6
Read grant proposals, 28, 37
Reader, 23
   responsibilities, 27
Read-in Foundation, 14
Reading teacher, 49
Reasons for rejection, 75
Record keeping, 88
Records, 88
Recycle, 78
Reading loft, 7
Redundancy, 57, 63
Rejection, 74-75, 78
Relationships, 13, 18, 89-90
Reports
   final, 51, 88-89
   fiscal, 53
   interim, 51, 88, 90
Reporting, 88
Request for proposal (RFP), 21, 29
Research or researching, 10, 12, 13, 15, 41
   organizing, 12, 22
Researcher, 29
Resubmit, 75, 78
Resume, 4, 9, 24, 26, 28, 48, 71, 118
Reviewing grants, 24
   state grants, 25
   federal grants, 26
Revise, 66, 72
Rewrite, 62, 65

Right align, 61
Right Grant Online, 16
Rocking chair, 7
Rotary International, 86
Rubric, 25-28, 61

S

Salaries, 46
Sample grant proposals, 54, 117
Sample resume, 118
Schematics, 25, 52
School board, 47, 85
School Library Journal, 17
School of Management and
   Administrative Services, 20
Scoring rubric, 25-28
Scrapbook, 82-83
Search, 17
   tips, 17
   Web, 17
Seminar, 19, 77
Sertoma International, 13
Service learning, 56
Seventh Mental Measurement Yearbook, 50
Shawnee Mission Education
   Foundation, 25, 131
Shelving, 7
Signature(s), 32, 34, 53, 70-72
Site visit(s), 51, 89
Social Security, 47
Sophocles, 81
Spacing, 29, 33, 61
Special collections, 6
Special education, 56
Special Population (LSTA)
   grants, 15
Special programs, 7
Specificity, 59
Spreadsheet, 46
Standards, 44

State, 86
  ally, 21
  committee, 24
  grants, 25
  humanities councils, 15
  libraries, 15, 21
  purchasing guidelines, 30
Statement of need, 41
Statistical Abstract of the United States, 17
Statistician, 29, 67
Statistics, 18, 29, 42, 60, 63, 88
Student outcomes, 42
Style, 58
  guide, 68
SUMI Library Foundation, 43
Summative evaluation, 49
Summer institute, 78
Superintendent of Documents, 16
Superintendent, 5, 28, 30, 32, 47, 52, 53, 70, 71, 81, 82
Support letters, 52
Supporting documentation, 53
Sustainability, 52
Synonyms, 57, 68

T

3M, 14
  3M Professional Development Grants, 14
Table of contents, 41, 62
Tables and chairs, 7
Target audience, 51
  population, 18
Task force reports, 42
Tax-exempt status, 71
Teach, 85
Teacher Quality Enhancement Grant Program, 26
Team, 14, 27, 28
Technical Development Corporation, 20
Technology
  evaluation, 49
  inventory, 130
  manufacturers, 15
  plan, 5, 71
Technology Today, 17
Test resources, 50
Testimonial, 67, 71
Thank-you note, 13, 74, 78
Thesaurus, 68
Thoreau, Henry David, 33
Time-and-task, 60
Timeline, 5, 44, 51
Title, 46, 65, 72
  page , 40
To do list, 38
Tone, 68
Transition words, 58-59
Travel, 45
Type faces, 30
Type size, 29, 30, 62
Types of grants, 13
  foundations, 13

U

U.S. Department of Education, 26, 37
  Office of Educational Research and Improvement, 50
  Office of Post Secondary Education, 26
  Teacher Quality Enhancement Grant Program, 26
  Technology Programs, 103

V

Veteran, 30
Vision, 2, 5, 8, 43, 75
Visualization, 3
Voice of Youth Advocates, 18
Voice, 30, 58
Volunteer, 5, 24-27, 32, 85

W

Weak writing, 76
Web, 19
White space, 61
Workshop(s), 8, 19, 37, 51, 76